More
than These

"Much we hold dear are things that God has given to us to care for and use for His glory." But do we love God "more than these"? June Kimmel strives to answer this question from John 21 as she reflects on things she has loved more in her own life—family, friends, job, home, security. Take a look deeper for yourself as June demonstrates how to love God "more than these." With insightful study questions at the end of the book, this book will help you understand why Jesus asked Peter this question and why He asks the same question of you and me. I was humbled by the poignant questions she asked and found myself reflecting on my own answers. This is a must-read for any Christian—whether you have been saved for a minute or fifty years.

—KATIE CRUICE SMITH

Author of *Why Did You Choose Me?* and upcoming release, *Children of the Promise: Adoption Through the Bible,* a Bible study for adoptive families

More than These

A Woman's Love for God

June Kimmel

Ambassador International

GREENVILLE, SOUTH CAROLINA & BELFAST, NORTHERN IRELAND

www.ambassador-international.com

More Than These

A Woman's Love for God

ISBN: 978-1-62020-803-8
eISBN: 978-1-62020-806-9

Unless otherwise marked, Scripture quotations taken from the King James Version, The Authorized Version. Public Domain.

Cover Design & Typesetting by Hannah Nichols
Ebook Conversion by Anna Riebe Raats

AMBASSADOR INTERNATIONAL
Emerald House
411 University Ridge, Suite B14
Greenville, SC 29601, USA
www.ambassador-international.com

AMBASSADOR BOOKS
The Mount
2 Woodstock Link
Belfast, BT6 8DD, Northern Ireland, UK
www.ambassadormedia.co.uk

The colophon is a trademark of Ambassador

To the ladies of Faith Baptist Church
With my love and gratitude
For the precious time we have shared
Growing in grace
And
In the knowledge of
Our Lord and Savior.

Contents

CHAPTER 1

My Love Tested

THE PAST MONTHS WERE AN emotional blur. The necessary tasks to make plans turn into reality crowded out our normal routine. I looked and asked myself, "How did we get to Wisconsin?"

I had to begin to sort not just the boxes waiting to be unpacked, but also all the recent events, and put this roller coaster into a perspective that would hopefully give God the glory He deserves.

A number of years ago our family moved to South Carolina for a time of refreshment and restoration. We intended to return to full-time ministry within a short time. The Lord had us there longer than we had planned.

During those years, we stayed busy serving, teaching, and counseling in our local church. Our daughters graduated from college and were married, and our son was almost finished with college. It was during this time that I began my writing. We accomplished much and served many, but my husband never lost the drive to be back in full-time service.

David began to circulate his name with a ministerial recommendation service. The director had advised him to send a resume, cover letter, and a referral letter from our pastor to the churches of interest. One of the dozen packets we put together went to a church in Wisconsin.

Within a short time, communication began between Dave and several of the churches. After a doctrinal statement and an additional questionnaire, the church in Wisconsin called. Soon we were on our way with my husband as an official pastoral candidate. That weekend

9

visit had shown us that the Lord was orchestrating all the details. Our lives were about to drastically change.

The November weekend quickly turned into a January move. After more than eleven years in the South, we packed our things and left our three children, two sons-in-law, two granddaughters, and our church family.

Who moves to Wisconsin from South Carolina in January? Only someone who was following God's call. For the first time in my life, I realized my definition of obedience was inadequate for what I was facing.

My excitement was genuine as we anticipated the new ministry, but the agony of my heart overwhelmed and overshadowed what the Lord was giving us. Our son was leaving for Spain to study for the semester. When he returned in June, we would be gone. Our daughters and their families would no longer be nearby. The thoughts of the many miles that would separate us seemed to crush my grieving heart. Yet I knew this was God's call. There was no option but to follow.

I turned to the Bible, and there in His love and faithfulness God met me. I knelt before Him in surrender, and I cried out for comfort. He led me to John 21:15 and to the question that He had asked Peter so long ago: *"Lovest thou me more than these?"*

I knew God was asking for my answer to Peter's question. Who did I love most? My children, granddaughters, present ministry, or Him?

I began to search God's Word and the depths of my heart to find the answer. He was asking for my total commitment to the ministry we were embarking upon. How could I give that kind of dedication with so much of my heart left in the South?

My own words seemed to haunt me as I faced this personal query. When I speak to ladies across the country, I often challenge them to surrender completely to God's will for their lives. One of my books is titled *A Life Surrendered*.

I was familiar with the dedication that God expects of us. He displayed for us the ultimate example of surrender when He left the glories of heaven to come to this earth as our Savior. I recalled a specific "Life Surrendered" seminar that I taught in northeastern Pennsylvania. In a session entitled "A Life Surrendered in His Hand," I used the illustration of the vine and branches (John 15) to picture the removal of things in our lives that hinder us from bearing the fruit God desires.

My own heart was challenged while I spoke that day—challenged to consider my response if the Lord would someday call us away from our family. My voice wavered as I cut a section off the vine to illustrate the surrender needed for separation. Our first granddaughter was due in a few months. How tempted would I be to refuse to move? My soon-to-be-a-grandma's heart had found that question troubling. Two years later, the occasion and the question became real.

Did I love the Lord more than anyone or anything else? Was I willing to go?

I'd like to share my pilgrimage with you. In the chapters that follow, I'll recount the lessons that this question and this event have taught me. While you walk this journey with me, please consider your answer to the Savior's question, "Lovest thou me more than these?"

CHAPTER 2

Lovest Thou Me?

WAITING IS NOT SIMPLE. IT demands a discipline only achieved during the course of the wait. How much easier it is to be busy! Time passes quicker with an abundance of activities, but waiting is a totally different process. When you wait you may grow impatient as the time passes without sign of progress and you may begin to question if God will use you again.

Some may doubt our obedience and surrender to God's will. The dubious eye of the pious may challenge or misjudge our motives. Waiting leads to God's solution and not our own when we genuinely wait on Him.

That's how God worked in my life. The many years of waiting on God's next ministry for us were not wasted. As we faithfully served, He was preparing our hearts for the full-time ministry He had awaiting us. Without the years of waiting, we wouldn't have been ready to answer the question that so clearly distinguished this new call.

The Lord Jesus asked Peter, *"Lovest thou me more than these?"* on the beach that early morning, and so He asked of me: Was I willing to obey? Did I love Him more? More than anything or anyone else?

Many have had to answer this question with a cost far greater than mine. The searching, however, was the same. Who was first in my life? What limit was I placing on my surrender? Without the years of waiting, the answer might have been much different. The Lord knew when His lessons were complete. In His time, He asked the question. His question demanded an answer.

SETTING THE SCENE

After the resurrection of the Lord Jesus, the disciples waited for their instructions. What were they to do now that the Savior had risen? He told them to wait. They didn't know for sure what they were waiting for, but they knew that the Lord could be trusted. Wait they must. But their impatience demanded action. They turned to what they knew. They went fishing.

I don't think they really wanted to fish. After three years at Jesus' side ministering to the multitudes, this may have been the last thing they wanted to do. Yet, in this time of waiting, they returned to the familiar. Many have criticized the disciples for their decision, but it was in this time of the mundane that the Lord Jesus directed them to their ultimate mission—to love Him above all and be only fishers of men.

In John 21, Peter and several of the disciples left their waiting to spend the night fishing on the Sea of Galilee. The long night left them weary and unrewarded; they caught no fish. These disappointed fishermen headed to land. Through the first hint of morning light, they saw the form of a man on the shore. They were unable to identify this shadow. No doubt there was something familiar about Him.

How often do we fail to see the presence of the Lord as we struggle with the uncertainties of life? His presence is there, but we find it difficult to recognize Him. The cares of this world shadow our view, yet He is there. He never leaves our side. He is completely aware of all that we are facing. We may not realize it is Him, but He never leaves us or forsakes us.

Jesus dearly loved the disciples. When the little vessel got closer to shore, the Stranger inquired, "Children, have ye any meat?" Calling them "children" was a term of endearment or tenderness showing His affection and concern for these fishermen, His friends. How humbling it must have been for these seasoned fishermen to admit their efforts had been in vain.

Is someone you know a fisherman? Your husband, friend or sister? How does that person respond when you ask about the day's catch? If nothing is caught, no one is happy!

There is a man in our church who loves to fish in Lake Michigan or one of the smaller lakes in our area. He has asked the men in my family to join him on several fishing expeditions. On some of these adventures, my husband never caught a single fish. Why get up at 3:00 a.m., take all that gear, bait, and poles to go sit in a boat in the middle of a lake with no guarantee of bringing home a fish?

It's a sad day indeed when a fisherman comes home with no fish. The tales of the open sea lose all their intrigue without the catch!

In the middle of this sad exchange, the disciples learn there is still hope. In John 21:6, Jesus directed the men to cast their net on the right side of the boat. Who else but Jesus would give them such specific instructions? Apparently someone standing on the shore of the Sea of Galilee could actually see schools of fish swimming. The disciples perhaps thought that this stranger was seeing what they could not. The disciples did as he said. They cast their net on the right side and their catch was amazing. With the abundant catch, the disciples immediately recognized the One on the shore to be the Savior.

Peter wrapped his coat around himself, dove into the water and swam to shore as friends from nearby boats helped retrieve this amazing catch. A night of failure ended with a marvelous catch of one hundred fifty-three great fish. When the disciples reached the shore, they saw the fire, the fish, and the bread.

Jesus had prepared breakfast for His servants to show His unending care and provision. His disciples recognized their continued dependence on the Lord. The Master had not come to buy their fish but to supply their need—breakfast. Jesus "becomes once more their Host and their Minister . . . . He attends to their requirements. He feeds them from this strangely bestowed supply . . . . He inspires their methods. He shares in their victory, after painful fruitless toil."[1]

Because He is God, He could have the men catch a multitude of fish at sunrise after a long night of no success. Because He is the God-man, He could join the disciples and eat a wonderful breakfast.

With the disciples' physical needs met, the stage was set for Jesus to ask Peter this important question. John 21:15 says, "So when they had dined, Jesus saith to Simon Peter . . . Lovest thou me more than these?"

When we consider this exchange between Peter and the Lord Jesus, we must ask ourselves this same question. What place does Jesus truly have in our hearts? Our response to the details of this conversation will reveal our love for the Lord Jesus.

PERSONAL EXCHANGE

The events of the past weeks impacted each person at this gathering. First, there was the Lord Jesus. In spite of the cruelty and suffering of His passion and crucifixion, Jesus remained unchanged. In His tenderness, He called the disciples His children (John 21:5). His manner expressed an unrelenting love and thoughtfulness (John 21:9). His disposition continued to be gracious and kind, and yet unwavering (John 21:12).

Today He is still concerned for the temporal as well as the spiritual needs of each of us. We serve and pray to this same Master. Some of us often think that had we been with the disciples and seen Jesus face-to-face, it would be easier to trust Him. Be assured, dear friend, our Lord is the One who stood on the shore of Galilee that day. He is unchanged!

Peter, however, had drastically changed from the day Jesus first called him away from the fishing nets. Walking with the Lord Jesus had transformed Peter. Peter loved Jesus and had faithfully followed Him, but when Jesus faced His darkest hour, Peter denied that he knew Him despite his promise to follow the Lord whatever the cost. After all Peter had learned and experienced by Jesus' side, after all the love the Lord had shown him, Peter declared he didn't even know who the Lord Jesus was. While he warmed his hands by the fire, Peter cursed and swore that he did not know Him. With the last word barely across his lips, Peter heard the cock crow, fulfilling the Lord's prediction. Peter realized what he had done. The one who had boasted of unwavering loyalty to the Master had just denied Him.

On the shore that day, we recognize that Peter had changed. When the Lord questioned Peter's love, Peter's thoughts probably replayed his traitorous acts of that crucifixion night. Before the Lord could really use Peter, Peter's pride needed crushed, his self-confidence shattered, his boldness tempered, and his words guarded. Jesus called Peter "Simon" his original name and not "Peter" which means "rock." Peter was exactly what God wanted him to be—humble. God could now rebuild Peter into someone He could mightily use.

God still works in a similar way today in our lives. He takes us and shatters who we are. God reveals who we think we are, and then shows us that we are nothing without Him. We often go screaming and fighting all the way to that humility; but, when our lessons are complete, He begins to rebuild us piece by piece. He makes us into who He wants us to be for His glory!

The other disciples that had been fishing with Peter were also at this breakfast. They listened as Jesus asked Peter this sobering question. They had abandoned the Lord Jesus the night of His arrest and trial. When they heard the Lord ask Peter this question, they may have wondered if the Lord would turn and ask them to answer as well. What explanation could they possibly give? They had abandoned Jesus when He needed them. Perhaps they thought that Peter's answer would give them a clue about how to reply.

PIERCING QUESTIONS

While Jesus looked into Peter's eyes, His words probably pierced to the depths of Peter's soul and revealed his heart. The Lord asked Peter this profound question so that Peter could search his heart and see the depths of his love for the Savior. Jesus challenged Peter with the need for unswerving devotion by repeatedly asking Peter if he loved Him.

The Lord didn't ask Peter how much he adored or feared Him. He didn't ask Peter about his faith or about his service. Peter would have preferred those questions. And wouldn't we?

We could enthusiastically tell of our activities. After all, some of us cook good meals for our family. Some of us teach Sunday school. Some of us help our neighbor. Some of us sing in the choir. Our list of ministry no doubt would impress.

But the Lord asked Peter to look deep inside his heart and evaluate his love.

In verse 15, Jesus asked, "Simon, lovest (*agapao*) thou me more than these?" The Lord used the word for *love* which is *agape*—the highest, most perfect kind of love, a divine love. Peter answered, "Yea Lord thou knowest that I love thee." Peter's word for *love* (*phileo*) here is a strong, affectionate friendship love, a bond of fond affection. Peter's choice of words revealed his reluctance to claim the supreme dedication that his life had not supported.

The second question the Lord Jesus presented Peter is in verse sixteen. Jesus uses *agape* again, but this time the question is shorter and without comparisons—"lovest thou me?" With this question Jesus inquired about the very existence of Peter's love. Peter again answered with the friendship love that he had used for his first answer.

The third time, Jesus uses Peter's word *phileo* in this final inquiry in John 21:17. Peter was grieved because Jesus now asked with the word for friendship love which signified less than total devotion. The Lord Jesus questioned the existence of this lesser level of love that Peter had thought safe to claim. In essence, the Lord asked if Peter even loved Him with human affection.[2]

Peter's answers give us insight into his heart; he was humbly searching for a proper understanding of his love for the Savior. He knew it was not trustworthy to rely on what he had said or done to show or prove his love. So Peter appealed to an omniscient, all-knowing, God. God the Son did not need Peter's self-acclaimed declaration of love. The Lord Jesus already knew the love that ruled Peter's heart.

What does Peter's question-and-answer session teach us? The Lord Jesus asked Peter this question to challenge us to search our hearts to see the depths of our love for Him. If our love for God is little, other areas in our lives will reflect the same. When Charles Spurgeon preached a sermon on this passage, he clearly stated that our love for God determines every area of our lives. He said, "If love be little, fear will be little, and courage for God will be little; and whatsoever graces there be, though faith lieth at the root of them all, yet do they so sweetly hang on love, that if love be weak, all the rest of the graces most assuredly will be so"[3]

What is our love for God like? His love is so magnificent that our words fail to declare its greatness. It is a sacrificial love demonstrated by His surrender to die on the cross for our sins. He literally gave His life for us. Yet the Lord asks us to compare our love for Him to His amazing love for us. How do we match up?

No matter how long our resume of ministries may be *without* the proper love our actions are valueless. In fact, love is the foundation of all we do. In 1 Corinthians 13, we are told that even though we may speak with the tongues of men and of angels, have the gift of prophecy, understand all mysteries and all knowledge, have a faith that could remove mountains, give all our goods to feed the poor, and give our bodies to be burned, these extraordinary works are worthless without love.

That's why it is crucial to ask ourselves this piercing question: "Do we love the Savior?" Without love, our good efforts are empty and hollow. We are useless and unprofitable if our service, however noble, is done without a supreme love for God. The magnitude of our love is crucial in God's economy.

PERSONAL ANSWERS

In each exchange in John 21, Peter answers with the same phrase. "Yea, Lord; thou knowest that I love thee." When Peter gave the answer to the final question, he added these words, "Lord, thou knowest *all* things" (emphasis added). Peter responded with new understanding. He was not trying to defend his love. Through the experience of denying the Lord and receiving God's forgiveness, he realized he didn't have to defend his previous actions and words. He responded instead with, "Lord, you already know what kind of love is in my heart." Peter looked to the omniscience of the Lord to understand.

According to John 2:25, Jesus knows what is in man. By his answer, Peter declared his comprehension of grace—he didn't deserve God's love and forgiveness, but God had given him both. With that understanding of grace, Peter was humbled.

Now we must take a sincere look at our hearts. What would our answer be if Christ asked us this question: "Lovest thou me more than these?"

Could we answer as Peter did? Our all-knowing, all-wise Lord knows what love for Him we possess. Would we feel compelled to defend or describe our love for the Lord? Could we with Peter's humility and confidence answer, "Lord, You know!" However we would answer, He already knows our heart!

God knows if we have recognized that we fall short of His perfection. He knows if we've received His precious gift of salvation or if we still need to reach out and receive this gift. God also knows if we are in love with the Savior. He knows if our ultimate goal is to sit at His feet or if it is to impress others.

In Psalm 139:23-24, the psalmist prays, "Search me, O God, and know my heart: try me, and know my thoughts: and see *if there be any* wicked way in me, and lead me in the way everlasting."

You and I should ask daily for God to search us and show us what love we have for Him. Please let me challenge you, friend. Ask God to reveal your heart as you continue reading the pages of this book.

Picture a heart-shaped box covered with shiny red wrapping paper. A quick shake of the box reveals that something is inside, but the ribbon-secured lid seals the box, hiding the contents. I can explain what is in the box in great detail. I can paint the most beautiful word pictures that my imagination could muster. You might get a glimpse of the enclosed objects in your mind's eye; but to really know for sure what it contains, you need to take off the lid and look inside. Our all-knowing God, dear friend, already knows what is in your heart! We can make the outside of our lives sparkle so brightly that those around us assume that the inside is as brilliant as the outside. We can give impressions that astound the most skeptical; but I must remind you, man looks at the outward appearance, but God sees the heart (1 Samuel 16:7). What's the love of your heart? God desires your honest answer.

TO KNOW GOD'S LOVE

Peter's heart must have been overwhelmed when Jesus questioned his love. For three years Peter had closely followed the Lord Jesus. Each message and miracle had been received and observed. Peter was keenly aware of Jesus' love for the multitudes and even more mindful of Jesus' love for him. When Peter verbalized the confusion and doubt that sometimes plagued his puzzled heart, Jesus always answered him with truth and compassion even when reprimand was needed. In spite of Peter's doubts and questions, Jesus' love for him was unwavering.

For us to accurately evaluate our love for the Lord, we need to consider His love for us. 1 John 4:10 puts the emphasis on the perfect love of God. "Herein is love, not that we loved God, but that he loved us and sent His Son to be the propitiation for our sins."

Our love is minute when compared to God's great love for us. The genuine picture of pure love is found only in God and perfectly demonstrated on the cross. Whenever tempted to doubt God's love for us, we only need to look to the cross to see the depths of His love vividly displayed and demonstrated.

CHAPTER 3

More Than These?

WITHIN THE FIRST SIX MONTHS of moving to Wisconsin, all of our children and my husband's parents came to visit. How strange it felt to have them visit our new world. Our son, Jon, summed it up well when he said it was extremely bizarre to travel all the way to Wisconsin and to realize this was now our home.

What fun we had showing them the places that had begun to hold new memories for us: the parks, the Lakeshore, the red barns and dairy cows, the antique shops on Mill Street, and most of all our new church family. Our children seemed genuinely eager to experience our new life when we shared these spots with them.

The eager acceptance that we saw between our church family and our children was precious. The women welcomed my daughters and granddaughters with a warm and loving response that was not unlike the one they had given me. The men eagerly welcomed my son, sons-in-law, and father-in-law by inviting them in such activities as fishing, hockey watching, foam ball, soccer, and eating burgers. Schedules did not allow all the ideas to happen this trip, so promises of more fun awaited future visits. All exceeded the expected cordiality. Our little town felt another step closer to really being home.

The hardest part of the visits was the inevitable finale—their de-parture. When the day for the plane ride home drew near, the wound in my heart that I thought was healing re-opened. The agony of giving hugs and kisses at the airport devastated me. With the anticipation of the departure, the pain started the day before they were to leave. More tearful good-byes. More long walks to the car from the terminal followed by sad miles driving back home. More silence as we walked in the door of our house—the noisy fun of family gone.

I've asked some more experienced in this practice of good-byes if it would get easier. Their answers have given me no hope of relief. They say it will continue. But so will God's grace!

I've claimed His grace often in the past. Grace for graduations, for wedding, for sickness, for decisions, and scores of other life-changing events. Now I'm finding that God's grace is sufficient for separation—perhaps the biggest test yet.

I've found myself continuing to return to the question that Jesus asked Peter there on the shores of the Sea of Galilee. "Lovest thou me more than these?" I must ask myself once again; do I love Him more than anyone or anything else? Do I love Him enough to serve with an attitude of joy and a spirit of humility while far from those I love? It would be easy to serve with resentment, bitterness, or with a heart of pride for the great sacrifice that I think I'm making. Is that the service that He desired? No. If I love Him more than these, I will serve with a gracious, sacrificial joy that only God can give.

John 21:15: *So when they had dined, Jesus saith to Simon Peter, Simon, son of Jonas, lovest thou me more than these? He saith unto him, Yea, Lord; thou knowest that I love thee. He saith unto him, Feed my lambs.*

Peter stood on the shores of the Sea of Galilee when the Lord asked him three times, "Lovest thou me?" This question demanded that Peter look to the depths of his heart to evaluate his love for the Savior. Peter's question became ours when we considered what our response would be. The Lord knew what love was in Peter's heart and He knows what kind of love is in ours. We must contemplate the second and possibly harder part of this question.

The first time that Jesus asked Peter this question, He included a comparison—"Lovest thou me more than these?" Jesus was asking Peter to compare his love for Him to his love for other things in his life. What are your "these?" Yours are probably different than mine.

But all of us have good, God-given things or people in our lives that we are tempted to love with a love that only the Lord deserves.

HIGHEST LOVE

Peter by profession was a fisherman. Just a few hours earlier Peter had returned to fishing while he waited for directions from the Lord Jesus (John 21:3). With this tremendous catch of fish safely brought to shore, the Lord may have been asking Peter, "Do you love your fishing—your job, your past—more than you love Me?" Jesus may have been calling Peter to love Him enough to forsake all he was familiar with and be exclusively devoted to fishing for men.

Jesus was possibly asking Peter, "Do you love Me more than these other disciples love Me?" This piercing question reminded Peter that he had promised to never forsake the Lord no matter what happened, even if everyone else abandoned Him. Although the other disciples fled, Peter's attempt to follow the Savior led him to a place of denial. He failed to keep the promise of loyalty that he had made. How did his love for the Lord compare to the other apostles' love for the Savior? How does Peter's love or my love compare to the love that God expects?

Mark 12:30 states, "And thou shalt love the Lord thy God with all thy heart, and with all thy soul, and with all thy mind, and with all thy strength: this *is* the first commandment."

Jesus proclaimed that our love for Him must exceed our love for all else. Jesus requires His servants to possess a supreme love for Him. The busyness that describes our days does not impress God. The flurry of activities that fill the lives of many Christians does not indicate the depth of their love for God. The Savior wants us busy about His business, but not at the expense of growing in our love for Him. God wants a 100% of who we are with a 100% of our love. When we love Him supremely, all the other people and things in our lives fall into their proper place.

In Luke 14:26, Jesus explained that if our love for those dearest to us do not seem like hatred in comparison to our love for Him, our love was not what He desired. "If any man come to me, and hate not his father, and mother, and wife, and children, and brethren, and sisters, yea, and his own life also, he cannot be my disciple." Would you describe your love for the Savior to be above your love for all others? No matter how noble and precious our loved ones are, God alone deserves our highest love.

We must carefully and prayerfully examine our lives lest we miss the true love of our heart. We have to begin with an honest assessment to determine our highest love, and then humbly trust and surrender to the teaching of God's Word to truly love Him above all else.

HONEST ASSESSMENT

When Jesus asked Peter this question, He demanded an honest answer. Jesus desired only the truth. Our world has become extremely forgiving of dishonesty. To tell the truth has become an option not a way of life. In the past, commitment and honesty accompanied a man's word. A verbal promise was as binding as a signed and notarized contract. However, today even those in public office seem to have no problem saying what they feel will be to their best advantage, true or not. However, the politicians are not exclusive in their condoning of altering the truth. The vast majority of Americans admit to lying in a variety of situations if the truth would be hurtful to others, especially to people they love the most. Lying has become an accepted part of everyday life for many.

The Lord clearly gave us His view of lying in the account about Ananias and Sapphira (Acts 5). The early church was growing rapidly and many of these early believers were making great sacrifices to meet the church's needs. Some of the believers were selling their property and giving the profits to the church. In an attempt to gain respect, Ananias and his wife devised a plan. When their property sold, they kept a portion and gave the rest to the church, but told the church leaders that their gift was the total of their sale. Within the next few hours, both Ananias and Sapphira were dead and buried. Their lie was an abomination to a holy God.

Although God does not deal as quickly with lying in our present world, He still finds it repugnant. Our deceptive answers may fool our inquirers, but not God. When He asks us, "Do you love me more than these?" He's not looking for the right answer; He is looking for the truth.

We must honestly face our heart's condition. Are we loving God more than all else? Or are we just saying the expected to win spiritual respect from those around us? Are we trying to impress God? God regards our lies as He did Ananias' and Sapphira's lies. We should desire to be honest before the Lord in our assessment of our heart's desire. Do we truly love Him more than all else? We must keep our focus on Him and allow Him to increase our love for Him. Growing is difficult if we are struggling to admit our need. We must honestly evaluate our heart to accurately understand our love for Him.

HUMBLE TRUST

Jesus also demands a total trust from His followers. Trust and supreme love are inseparable in God's eyes. Psalm 2:12b states, "Blessed are all they that put their trust in Him." When we love the Lord more than anything or anyone, we place our complete confidence in Him. We lay at His feet every burden and need. We roll on Him the details of our life and find that He accepts them all whatever their significance. In Him, we find our refuge and safety in the midst of any storm. He willingly allows us to lean on His amazing strength and to rest confidently in His wisdom and love. We stand securely on the promises and truths of His Word. In His presence, we find strength.

In Habakkuk 2:4b, God tells the prophet that "the just shall live by his faith." The unknown and unexplainable reveal our confidence or faith in God. In spite of the circumstances, God wants us to walk with unquestioning confidence in Him. We long for explanations that God is not obligated to give. These times of silence reveal most clearly our trust, our faith. 2 Corinthians 5:7 states, "For we walk by faith, not by sight." Our love for God is measured by our humble trust when the circumstances of life are the most demanding.

HOLY SURRENDER

Total trust leads to total commitment that brings Him glory in everything we do every moment of every day. Complete commitment will change how we wipe runny noses, do the laundry, answer the phone, or carry out our responsibilities at work. God deserves and desires our total unreserved surrender. It is easy to piously say, "Lord, I love you and I'm serving you," and then continue to control the rest of our lives without a thought to include Him. Struggles come when we let people, things, or responsibilities take our focus off of God. No matter what the distraction, keeping Him first is essential. Many times pride overtakes our heart as we compare our spirituality with that of someone else.

Anything we love more than God is an idol that must be dethroned. This superlative love requires a daily surrender to the Lord for Him to remove the idols from our hearts.

What idols are in your life? One idol is no less offensive to the Savior than another. In 1 John 5:21, John tenderly challenges, "Little children, keep yourselves from idols. Amen."

We probably don't have the statues or corner shrines in our homes that were common in Bible times and that are still in many countries today. Yet, all of us have idols that seek to capture our hearts. We recently discussed this topic in my women's Bible study class. As the women shared the things that can be idols in this 21st century, it became apparent that this is still a battle that we all face. Their answers included: jobs, money, possessions, prestige, and people. All of us have something or someone on the throne of our life. Is it God? Do we love Him with our greatest passion?

Many of us have defined idolatry in terms of things around us instead of recognizing it as an issue of our sinful heart. Idols take our focus off of God and cause us to pursue what we believe to be essential. In these terms, we realize that Jesus asked Peter to carefully examine his heart and uncover the idols dwelling there. Whatever his "these" represented was vying for the priority of his life. Peter had to ask himself what he loved, desired, or feared more than God.

In many Old Testament accounts, we read of high places that were devoted to the worship of idols. Throughout the chronicles of the kings of Israel and Judah, God commanded His people to destroy the high places and worship only Him (2 Kings 12:3; 14:4; 15:4). When God's people disobeyed and left these areas intact, they were tempted to worship idols and forsake God. Sometimes the people would use these places to worship God, but as time passed they would try to worship God and maintain the idol worship as well (2 Kings 14-15). One king might destroy the high places and the next would rebuild them (2 Kings 18:4 and 21:3).

How often do we do the same? We know the blessings of loving and worshiping God as He would have us to; but we try desperately to live for Him and the world at the same time. Other times we simply forsake the Savior and restore the idols back to a place of prominence.

To love the Lord more than all else requires an abandonment of all idols and a surrendering of our hearts fully to Him and His control. In the following chapters, we will consider various aspects of our lives that may represent the idols with which we struggle. All of these things or people are important to us—ones that we dearly love or things we thoroughly enjoy; but they may have taken a place in our hearts that belongs only to God.

May our hearts be ready to lay on the altar of surrender whatever He shows us. Ask our gracious Lord to show you your need. He alone deserves first place in your life. Only He deserves your greatest love.

Let's return to our heart-shaped box that we pictured in the last chapter. Several ribbons encircle our beautifully wrapped box. While the box and its content illustrate what is in our hearts, we must deal with the ribbons that surround it to fully appreciate what is inside. Unless these ribbons are untied and removed the contents of the box will remain unknown. With the lid secure, the treasures inside are only speculation. We may be able to raise the lid slightly to catch a glimpse of what is inside; but no one will be able to see in the box completely. The three ribbons represent the three principles required for spiritually evaluating our hearts before God—honest assessment, humble trust, and holy surrender. If we refuse to confront our heart with an honest assessment based on God's Word, to humbly trust in our God who loves us perfectly, and to wholly surrender ourselves to God; we will never comprehend if we truly love God most.

GOD'S LOVE IS UNCONDITIONAL

Our love for others is often influenced by the circumstances between us. The closest of friends can face times of awkwardness in their relationships. Love between people is often based on what they do or on who they are. That love is conditional and often times selfish. Even love between parent and child can be destroyed because of disobedience, selfishness, or sinful choices.

God's love for us is perfect and holy because God *is* love.

1 John 4:8: *He that loveth not knoweth not God; for God is love.*

Romans 5:8: *But God commendeth his love toward us, in that, while we were yet sinners, Christ died for us.*

What a comfort to know that God's love is not dependent on us. There is nothing we can do to make God love us more. Neither is there anything we can do to make God love us less! There are no conditions or requirements that we must fulfill for God to love us. We don't have to make any promises or commitments to know His love. In fact, even though we are sinners, God loves us. Even though we are sinners, He sent the perfect, sinless Lord Jesus to die for our sins. His death demonstrates the greatest picture of love that He could show. This unconditional love is only found in God's love for us.

CHAPTER 4

More Than Family

WHEN WE MOVED TO WISCONSIN, we had two of the most adorable granddaughters in the world. Within our first year, a third granddaughter arrived. The two sisters lived in South Carolina and the third little doll lived in Tennessee. My oldest granddaughter, Ella, lived in South Carolina. Her quiet observation let nothing slip by. She shared with amazing clarity her unbelievable memory and detailed imagination. Her big blue eyes sparkled as she responded with clever wit to uncles who have taught her the art of teasing. She was a lover of people and playmates and outings to the zoo or park.

Ella called me one day. "Gram, Emery and I went on a bear hunt!"

I know that sounds silly, but this was a game she and her cousin, Karis, and I played. We sat on the steps at Ella's house and made a plan to hunt for bears! Whether stuffed bears or pretend ones the enthusiasm was the same. The utmost stealth and cunning led to an ending of squeals of joy at the moment of capture. How fun that she was teaching her little sister, Emery, this special game!

Emery was one sweet smile. Her greatest joy was to be in the middle of the action. Nothing was beyond her effort. Led by the determination to be wherever Ella was, she crawled and cruised early. Her accomplishments ended with a smile of victory with the goal attained. Her eyes sparkled with a sweet mischief that melted a grandma's heart.

Their cousin Karis had a charm that amazed all. Whatever the activity, she faced it with enthusiasm. Her mom and dad had taught her to carry on a conversation with the expertise lacking in many adults. At meals she often asked others if they've had a good day. When she accompanied her mother through a checkout line, she introduced herself to the cashiers and asked them their name. Her "Nice to meet you!" concluded the exchange leaving all within earshot smiling and astonished. Her imagination made every moment we were together a marvelous adventure.

These little cousins are opposites but the dearest of friends. These girls are a precious part of my life. I often placed pictures of the girls on my book table when I had book signings. I realized that no other grandma wanted to see pictures of my granddaughters. They had a wallet full of pictures of their own grandchildren. Oh, they may have politely look at mine, but rest assured their pictures were on the way out.

Until we moved to Wisconsin, I lived three minutes from Ella and Emery and just three hours from Karis. When I knew the Lord was calling us north, these little girls came immediately to my mind. My own children were going to be easier to leave behind than these granddaughters. Did I love them more than I loved God? Was I letting these precious little ones take the place in my heart that only God deserved? It was hard to leave them behind!

The need for my surrendered obedience was obvious. I had recently taught a Sunday school lesson on surrendering to obedience, and I found myself applying this biblical truth in another way. Not only was it God's plan for me to obediently serve Him in Wisconsin, it was also His plan for my granddaughters to have me in Wisconsin. That reality was a bit harder to accept. Why would God want these little girls to have me a thousand miles away? I'm not sure I've totally answered that question, but I'm resting in the promises of the Word—"All things work together for good" (Romans 8:28).

A phone call with Beth brought my feelings into perspective. When I shared my grief for the many miles that would separate me from these I dearly loved, my daughter's response challenged me.

"Mom, you raised us to go where God wants us to go! Why would you not go where God wants you to go?" What could I say? I loved these little girls just like you loved your dearest family members, but we cannot love them more than we love God. We cannot be the right kind of mother, aunt, sister, or daughter if we are not putting God first.

UNSELFISH SURRENDER

We saw in the last chapter the need to honestly assess our life, to humbly trust in the Lord, and to surrender completely all the idols of our heart. The pretty, respectable wrappings we have placed around our hearts need to be set aside to honestly reveal what resides within. Much we hold dear are things that God has given to us to care for and use for His glory. With each gift from His loving hand comes a responsibility. God wants us to be good stewards, someone who is entrusted to care for what belongs to another. We are to be faithful stewards of His precious gifts to us, but we are never to let those gifts become idols. Even His most precious gifts must occupy their proper place—behind our love for Him.

Our family is the most valuable gift that God gives us, so our greatest temptation may be to let these dear ones usurp the throne of our heart. God wants us to love our family, but our love for family must not supersede our love for Him.

UNCONDITIONAL RELEASE

Our perspective shapes what we think, see, and do. When we examine this principle closer, we should realize it applies to many areas of our lives. When two people disagree they each have their point of view. As a third party, we may see both sides which makes it difficult to arbitrate the needed resolution. How different it feels when we are one of the two who disagree. Our side seems obvious while our opponent's side looks obscure and slightly ridiculous. Perspective makes the difference.

This principle came to mind as I considered the aspect of releasing our family to God's will. Maybe you are not the one that is considering a change. Maybe your children want to serve the Lord in a state or country that seems on the opposite side of the earth (and literally may be). Are you willing to let them go for the Lord to use them as He sees best? Or do you love them with a selfish love that says they must stay close?

Many would claim to be eager for their children to go wherever God would lead them. Many Christian parents desired for their children to follow God's plan. Yet, when the time came to follow God's call, some parents' surrender of the child was with strings tethered to home dictating the radius in which the child must find the will of God. They didn't want those family gatherings inconvenienced with further travel or possibly someone missing the event. The grandchildren further away? Every mile mattered or did it?

Obedience means an unconditional release of a family member to the will of God. The parents open their hands and hearts freeing the child to go where God calls them regardless of the distance. Unconditional release is part of loving God for both the parent and the child. For children, it means that their love for God has no boundaries; their hearts are ready and willing to obey God's will no matter the cost, no matter the location.

For the parent, release means that their love for God includes trusting Him to care for their loved one. God's love for their child is greater than theirs. The parents can rest confidently in the unchanging love of God and can release their child to unconditionally obey God's will whatever the cost.

Letting go is another opportunity to demonstrate to God that we love Him more than all others. Our eyes may fill with tears at the mere thought of this separation, but our hearts should rejoice that our children are willing to go where God calls. How can we hesitate to accept God's plan for them? If we love Him "more than these" we will let go. Completely!

UNRESERVED DEDICATION

In 1 Samuel, we read the account of a mother, Hannah, who was willing to give her child to the Lord. Elkanah had two wives—Hannah and Peninnah. Difficult as it is to imagine sharing our husbands with another woman, in Bible times this often happened. Hannah, whose name means "grace," was probably Elkanah's first wife. Hannah had not been able to have children, but Elkanah loved her with a precious love and honored her with a double portion of his blessing.

Elkanah's second wife, Peninnah, was ruthless in her daily reminders of Hannah's childlessness. The Bible says she provoked Hannah severely, making Hannah's life miserable.

Hannah's heart was grieved and angry. Elkanah asked Hannah, "Am I not more precious to you than ten sons? Do I not shower you with extra blessings and devoted love?"

I can remember my husband teasing me with a similar question as we contemplated our move north. However, my husband's question was, "Am I not better to you than little granddaughters?" You can imagine the fun I had answering.

While Elkanah was sincerely trying to fill the gap in Hannah's life, her heart grieved over her consuming emptiness. Her husband's kind words brought her no solace. Her grief had reached the point of anguish.

If the story of Hannah ended here, we would assume that Hannah's love for a baby had taken an undeserved place in her heart. The constant barrage of mean comments from Peninnah kept her wounded heart continually in pain. The grief of barrenness consumed her and the thoughts of a child seized the throne of her heart. Nothing Elkanah could say or do could to deter her grief.

Hannah's story, however, does not end here. God did His gracious work in Hannah's life. Elkanah took his family to the temple on a regular basis. In 1 Samuel 1:9-18, we see that this year Hannah went with a special mission. After they had eaten, Hannah went to the temple and prayed begging the Lord for a son. If God would grant her this one request, Hannah promised she would give her son back to the Lord for His service, that he would be a Nazarite from the womb. With her prayer heard, she offered God the promised sacrifice from a heart of deep love and devotion.

Eli, the priest, interrupted her prayers and accused her of being drunk. She quickly clarified her petition. Without knowing the request but witnessing her fervency, Eli assured her that God would answer her prayer. With this pledge given, Hannah left the temple rejoicing. Although she had no baby in her arms, she left a different woman! Her sadness turned to joy. Hannah confidently rejoiced in God because He had heard her prayer and would soon send the answer.

Most of us probably prayed similar prayers as we carried our children those months of pregnancy. It's not uncommon for a mother to ask the Lord for His divine assistance, and then promise that the child will be dedicated to the Lord. Hannah's intent was far more sacrificial than most of our prayers. She meant a literal giving of her son to God's service!

In verses 19-21, Samuel was born. His name means "name of God" or "heard by God." God had heard her prayer. He had granted Hannah the longing of her heart—a son. Now it was time for Hannah to keep the promise that her request included.

With the baby in her arms, she faced the reality of the pledge she had made. How easy it would have been to adjust her plans. Doubts may have flooded her thoughts. What was he going to do without his mother? Didn't he need her just a little longer? Couldn't she give him to God in her heart? This new mother kept her promise to God. She cared for Samuel; she nursed him; after she weaned him, she took him to the temple to serve. Bible scholars say that Samuel could have been as young as two or three years old. His age may be uncertain, but by the customs of weaning, he probably would have been no older than five. Hannah took her little boy and his little coat that she had made for him and left him at the temple with Eli. She made him a new coat each year and brought it to him at her annual visit to the temple.

I am amazed as I consider Hannah's response to leaving this little one at the temple. In 1 Samuel 2, Hannah rejoiced in the Lord and gave God great glory. Could you praise God if you had just left your three or four year old son at the temple with an elderly priest? Instead of crying (like we may do when we leave our child for the first day of Kindergarten), Hannah traveled home rejoicing. God gave her the gift of a son and now she gave that precious gift back to Him. Little Samuel easily could have become Hannah's idol after waiting for him so long.

Our heart can be drawn away from the Lord by an inappropriate attachment to our children. Without genuine surrender, our love for family can take the place that our greater love for God should have. Consider the following statements to see if your children have become an idol in your heart.

- When I think more about my child than I think about my God, my child has become my idol.
- When I worry over my child rather than trusting God, my child has become my idol.
- When my actions are to please my child rather my God, my child has become my idol.
- When I fear my child more than I fear my God, my child has become my idol.
- When I choose a peaceful relationship with my child rather than disciplining them according to God's Word, my child has become my idol.
- When I obey my child's demands rather than God's, my child has become my idol.
- When I seek my happiness in my child rather than in God, my child has become my idol.

Hannah loved God more than she loved her family. In Philippians 4:13 we read, "I can do all things through Christ which strengtheneth me." With Samuel weaned, an incredible test of Hannah's love for God began. Through His grace, she was able to keep the promise she had made to God a few years earlier. God may not ask us to give our children literally to Him, but we need a willingness to send them *anywhere* to do *anything* that God calls them to do. God provides what we need for us to do what He asks us to do. That provision includes the releasing of our children to God's plan.

Do we love our families more than we love the Lord? Do we put them before the Lord and His desires and will for us? May we strive like Hannah to daily present our families to God in full surrender.

Throughout the Gospels, Jesus displayed His compassion and mercy in His response to the needs of people. When we choose to walk in obedience regardless of the cost, He blesses our surrender in unexpected ways that reveal His benevolence. For me it came in the form of technology.

I don't know who invented it, but I forever will be indebted to the computer genius that gave the world of Skype. Just a few short months ago I was totally ignorant of this means of communication. Between our move and our son going to Spain for a semester of college, I treasured this modern marvel. For absolutely no cost to operate and a very small price for equipment, I could talk to my family in South Carolina, Tennessee, and Spain. Not only could I talk to them, I could see them! For this Gram/Mom, our internet chats have been an unexpected blessing.

I enjoyed the after-nap snacks that my little Ella and Karis enjoy. While they sat in their booster seats and ate, I visited with them. The news may be a new word they were saying or a new place they had been. I watched them color pictures and watched them play with their toys.

With the webcam strategically placed they shared the fun of lining up the people or cooking "mouse soup." New toys, games, and puzzles became a part of my world as they showed me the pieces as they played.

The real question was not whether I enjoyed my time watching them. The important question was, "Do they see me? Do they feel a connection to my world and to my heart?"

We bonded a little more each visit. My heart was thrilled to know they were disappointed if we lost connection.

Ella would declare, "Oh, we lost her!" when the monitor went blank.

The greatest treat was when they asked for me to read to them. I read to them on some of the earliest Skype calls. I chose books that they remembered us reading together before we moved. Now both girls would ask me to read to them and would tell me which books they wanted to hear. With their eyes glued to the computer, I held the pages up for them to see the pictures. Now our favorite read-to-me time has been stretched across the miles thanks to Skype.

Karis was actually more interactive with me than Ella for quite a while. She would sit on her mother's lap with her big brown eyes fixed on the computer. When she got her little pink glasses at fifteen months, she held them up to the camera for me to get a good look at them. I heard her first words via Skype. Her vocabulary exploded and with each call I shared those recently learned, meaningful sounds. It's priceless to see her little face light up to see me in my home in Wisconsin on her screen. Although she usually responds with, "Papa," I knew she was glad to see me, too.

And then there were the good-byes. Most Skype time ended with Gram getting kisses. They were not the slobbery ones that I would have received if we were together, but I still felt them as they put their little lips up to the computer or blew me a kiss.

Thank you, Lord, for giving me this way to talk to my little girls.

I enjoyed the times with their moms, dads, and uncle, but to "see" and "talk" to these little girls have made such a difference in keeping my heart submitted to serving the Lord so far away. The loneliness will still overwhelm me on some days, but thanks to Skype, my family was just as close as my computer!

Thank You, Lord, for bringing us to Plymouth. Thank you for the ties to the people's lives that I feel you stringing. My days are getting busy, but there's always time for a quick call. Thank you, Lord, for making Skype just for me.

GOD'S LOVE IS GIVING

John 3:16: *For God so loved the world, that he gave his only begotten Son, that whosoever believeth in him should not perish, but have everlasting life.*

This verse in John chapter three is among the most familiar of the entire Bible. The reference is often seen on signs at sporting events. The reference is recognized by masses of people, but the words and meaning are virtually unknown by the average fans.

God's great love for the world is declared with simplicity and clarity! God loves the world. His love extends to all of mankind. His love is not exclusive! No matter the country, the language, the skin color, or other distinguishing characteristics, God loves all. That universal love is shown in His giving!

God sent His Son to give His life for us on the cross. He knew we could never earn the forgiveness that our sinful hearts needed. He knew that only the Lord Jesus in His perfection and sinless life could successfully pay for our sins.

Because of His love, He gave the world the gift of salvation.

It's a joy to give someone a gift. When the gift is composed of something the other person desperately needs, the joy of giving is greater. God knew we needed Jesus. And because the Lord Jesus loves us so deeply, He willing came to this earth to be born in a manger and to die on our behalf.

We all have many people who we believe love us. God loves us so much that He gave Himself with the promise of an eternal life with Him if we but believe and call on His name!

Romans 5:8: *But God commendeth his love toward us, in that, while we were yet sinners, Christ died for us.*

CHAPTER 5

More Than Others-Friends

MOVING AWAY MEANT SAYING GOOD-BYE to friends at work. I had
been an adjunct instructor for over four years for the science center
that was part of our public school district. Although my position was
with the health education department, I had become acquainted with
almost every other aspect of the center. After the school year ended,
I helped teach and write programs for the summer science camps. I
also served as the director's assistant which took me all around the
hundreds of acres with messages and supplies. I learned the duties of
the welcome desks in two of the buildings. The news of my leaving
spread quickly throughout the departments to all my friends.

Their responses were surprising. Inquiries about the purpose of
our move followed their kind words. Their faces showed amazement
as I shared the news of my husband becoming the pastor of Faith
Baptist Church in Plymouth, Wisconsin. My southern friends could
not grasp the need to move a thousand miles away for him to pastor
a Baptist church when there were similar churches by the dozens in
every town within fifty miles. I could not deny how unnecessary the
move sounded, but I tried to use the opportunity to share the purpose
of following God's will wherever it might lead.

My last day and final classes at the science center was precious.
With classes concluded, we headed to lunch at a nearby restaurant.
The table in the private room was filled with dear friends, my co-
workers. Just being together one last time brought tears to my eyes.
As I looked around the table each chair was filled with a life that I
prayed I had touched for God's glory in some way. The scrapbook

of personal messages and photos and the other little gifts made my memories tangible.

When the ordered food was delivered, it crossed my mind that I should ask the Lord to bless this special lunch. What a perfect setting—our last time together with good food, pleasant conversation, and a moment of drawing attention to the goodness of God. I'm sure no one would have objected. But I didn't do it. I froze. I found no words to make the move to bring everyone's attention to a time of thanks. I cannot tell you how many times I've thought of that moment. It may sound excusable as you read this recounting of the incident. But in my heart I know that for that moment, after four years of trying to do just the opposite, I had let my love for these friends take precedent over my love for the Lord. My silence showed my heart's choice.

Family may be the most obvious group of people that we are tempted to love more than we love God. Hopefully the last chapter gave you an opportunity to analyze your family's role in your heart and put your relationship with the Lord above your family. Now we must consider another group of people that may be stealing your love from the Savior. Your friends and coworkers may have more influence in your life than you realize.

While at work, you may find it easier to be a silent witness and not boldly share Who you love and serve. Your personal life is easier to explain in terms the lost would understand instead of revealing your personal walk with the Lord. While among co-workers, you may not share that you are a Christian. For those hours of celebration or relaxation, you set aside your relationship with the Lord in an attempt to fit in. Your co-workers and friends may be silencing your witness. You may need to ask yourself, "Do I love the Lord more than I fear the opinions of these people in my life?"

THE PRAISE OF OTHERS

The approval of people around us can be of great importance to us. We can easily enjoy taking the glory for what we do instead of giving glory to God. The praise of others can often fill us with pride that overshadows our dependence on the Lord. Too often that praise feeds our ego and gives us motivation to do whatever is necessary to win the acclaim of others. Our love for such accolades can quickly surpass our love for God.

In John 12:42-43, we learn about a group of people who found it difficult to follow Jesus because they loved the praise of men. After hearing Him preach and teach, some of the chief rulers realized that Jesus was the long-awaited Messiah. Because of their fear of the Pharisees, they would not publicly acknowledge Jesus to be the Savior. Such an acknowledgement would forbid them from entering the synagogue. For a devout Jew, denial to the synagogue branded a person an outcast. The praise of the Pharisees and the Jewish community meant more to them than boldly following Christ.

In Acts 12:21-24, Herod loved the praise of men more than he loved God. The result of his pride was devastating. Between the verses in Acts 12 and the account of the Jewish historian Josephus, we learn Herod's demise. Herod proclaimed a feast day in honor of his advocate, the Roman emperor Claudius. Herod went before the mass of people in royal apparel. Josephus described his garment as one made of silver that glistened in the sun overwhelming the people. When he finished speaking the people chanted, "It is the voice of a god, and not a man." While they continued this shouting, an angel of the Lord struck Herod. Herod's choice to receive the glory that belonged only to God was a crime. Herod endured terrible pain for five days before he died; according to Josephus' account, worms ate at his dead body.

God is a jealous God according to Exodus 34:14, "For thou shalt worship no other god: for the LORD, whose name is Jealous, is a jealous God." God will not share His glory and worship with anyone or anything. When God gave Moses the Ten Commandments on Mount Sinai, the first two commandments clearly declared this truth.

Exodus 20:3-5b: *Thou shalt have no other gods before me. Thou shalt not make unto thee any graven image, or any likeness of any thing that is in heaven above, or that is in the earth beneath, or that is in the water under the earth. Thou shalt not bow down thyself to them, nor serve them: for I the Lord thy God am a jealous God.*

God's dealing with Herod may seem shocking and abrupt, but according to Romans 1, all that are guilty of not giving God the glory that He deserves will suffer the same condemnation. All who are ungodly (sin against God) and unrighteous (sin against others) will know the wrath of God. These individuals may have heard the truth yet chose to reject it and continue to serve the gods of this world. God holds each individual accountable without excuse. Countless people have given themselves and all glory to the gods of this world. Acts 12:32 concludes that all who give God's glory to anything or anyone other than God is worthy of death. All mankind apart from the Lord Jesus' saving grace falls into this category.

While the chief rulers and Herod loved the praise of men more than they loved and feared God, Peter exemplifies a man who loved God more than he loved praise. In Acts 10, we learn of Peter's call to go and preach to Cornelius. Although Peter hesitated at first to obey this difficult assignment, he obediently went to this Gentile home to present the good news of salvation (Acts 10:24). When Peter arrived, Cornelius fell down at Peter's feet, and worshiped him. Peter quickly lifted Cornelius up and told him to stand. Peter assured Cornelius that he was only a man and could not accept the honor that Cornelius was offering.

He had come to this home not to be worshipped, but to preach Christ who is the only One worthy of glory and praise. Peter refused this recognition because he loved God more than he loved the personal praise of men.

The flattery of others can eclipse the reality of our sinfulness.

How should we respond to accolades? Is it acceptable for us to give or receive complements given for achievement or ministry? We should encourage those around us as they serve by commending a job well done that brings God the glory. In fact, we should strive to develop the gift of encouragement in our daily lives. The difference comes from the response of the one receiving the encouragement. When praised, a person should turn the glory to the Lord. He alone is the source of all the good we do. He enables us and therefore should receive the honor! By sharing the words of encouragement, the person serving is blessed; they have given others opportunity to praise the Lord.

THE PERIL OF DENIAL—MATTHEW 10:32-33

Our love for friends can sometimes lead to a denial of the Savior, not through blasphemous words that deny a holy God but through our silence. When conversations and questions come by divine appointment we have a choice to make. Do we speak God's truth or respond with the generic, socially acceptable? The missed opportunities may even make us uncomfortable just not enough to seek forgiveness through confessing it as sin (1 John 1:9).

Our actions can also deny the Lord when they oppose the commands of a righteous God. Sometimes we ignore opportunities that would honor His precious name. How often do we leave circumstances untouched that were open doors to sharing the gospel? If they know we attend church regularly those around us have some biblical expectations of us. Denying God because we fear the thoughts, words, or opinions of those around us is far from insignificant to a holy God.

Confessing Him is to recognize that you are no longer your own but that you belong to the Lord Jesus. Jesus called all who followed Him during His earthly ministry to forsake all and to openly declare Him before others.

Matthew 10:32-33: *Whosoever therefore shall confess me before men, him will I confess also before my Father which is in heaven. But whosoever shall deny me before men, him will I also deny before my Father which is in heaven.*

Confessing Christ involves every area of our life. We should be "ashamed neither of the person, the character, the doctrines, nor the requirements of Christ."[1] If He truly has control of every aspect of our lives, we will emulate Him in our actions and acknowledge Him in every situation. We will recognize and share Him as Messiah when we submit to Him as our Authority in all issues of our heart and life.

When we fail to admit our relationship to the Lord Jesus before others, we are not only disobeying the Savior's direct command; but we are also refusing to plant the truth that God can use to help others trust Christ as Savior.

D.L. Moody once said, "When we have been washed in the blood of the Lamb, we get our mouths opened. We have to confess Christ here in this dark world and tell His love to others. We are not to be ashamed of the Son of God."[2] When we love the Lord more than anything or anyone, our lives and our words will reflect God's love. No fear will overshadow that love. We must daily keep our sin confessed and our heart surrendered to the Master. We who know Him as Savior should live boldly, obeying Him and sharing Him with others.

THE POWER OF SALT AND LIGHT

Although our love for the Lord is to be our greatest, we still have a responsibility to love those around us. In Matthew, our Savior compares Christians to salt and light. The smallest amount of salt makes a difference in whatever it touches and the greatest darkness cannot extinguish the tiniest light. Let's take a close look at salt and light to determine what our relationships with others should be.

SALT OF THE EARTH

Matthew 5:13a: *Ye are the salt of the earth.*

Salt is a picture of the believer's relationship to the world. The unique functions of salt describes what is necessary to meet the needs of mankind.

- Salt adds flavoring.

Psalm 34:8 says, "O, taste and see that the Lord is good." Psalm 119:103 further exclaims, "How sweet are Thy words to my taste." When used in the proper proportions, salt makes a difference in the outcome of the recipe. Have you ever forgotten to add the salt to a recipe? Cookie recipes often call for small amounts of salt—just a teaspoon or even less for dozens of cookies. Yet, if the salt is omitted the entire batch of cookies is inedible. The salt permeates the batter giving a favor that even the casual eater can detect. In the Christian life, we need to be salt. As salt, we give purpose to the mundane routines of everyday life. We flavor each task with an eternal impact when we walk close to the Lord and when He is our greatest love.

- Salt preserves.

In Genesis 18, we see the impact that righteous souls have in the evil world. When Abraham learned of Sodom's impending judgment, he attempted to negotiate an alternative to the destruction of this wicked city. Abraham pleaded with God to spare the city for the sake of the righteous people who were living there. If you read the account carefully, you learn that as few as ten righteous souls could have preserved the city. Even when we seem to have no influence, God knows our heart and our effort. Our witness and life may go unheeded by others, but it is not lost to an omniscient God. We may never know how our love for the Lord, when in its proper place, preserves the opportunity for the lost around us.

- Salt melts.

Walking on ice is much different than walking on snow. After nearly a dozen years in the South, I had to relearn the techniques for navigating in the snow and ice of Wisconsin. I quickly learned that there was a difference in crossing the two. The crunch of snow offered stability. The surface of ice offered none. Regardless of the tread of the sturdiest footwear, the threat of slipping was ever-present. Thankfully sprinkling a combination of salt and other chemicals on the area made it less slippery. While the winter sun shone on the treated area, the ice began to melt and walking became easier and safer.

God uses a Christian who walks as salt to melt the cold hearts of the lost in this wicked world. A loving, gracious witness can be a tool of the Holy Spirit to soften the heart of one who has resisted the gospel. The warmth of God's love in us turns away the bitterness and anger of a man running from the Savior.

My husband's uncle reminds of me of how God does His work in this way. For years this man would have nothing to do with God. He mocked my husband for his desire to serve the Lord. He rejected any attempt to share God's precious message of love and salvation. Even when his wife was dying with cancer, he politely but firmly stopped our attempts to share the gospel. As time passed, we realized that although he had silenced our witness, the Word we had shared continued to do its work in his heart. A few months after his wife died, he trusted Christ as Savior. He shared with us that the Lord began to melt his heart after one of the times he had stopped our witness. As the salt melts the patches of dangerous ice, God can use our surrendered lives to melt the cold hearts of the lost.

- Salt heals wounds.

Have you noticed the hurting people around you? People with burdens of varying proportions no doubt touch your life. Psalm 147:3 says the Lord, "healeth the broken in heart and bindeth up their wounds." For many years, salt has effectively treated wounds. Even today with all of modern medicine, a salt water solution is still a good option for disinfecting an area and helping prevent infection in a wound. When applied to the wound, the salt often stings, but the outcome usually is beneficial. As Christians, we have what the lost need to heal their wounded, sinful hearts. When we consistently love the Lord above all else, our words and actions stand ready to give the healing message of the gospel to those sin-sick souls around us.

When we read the rest of verse thirteen in Matthew 5, we learn that salt loses its benefits if it loses its flavor. In fact, this verses states that the salt "is thenceforth good for nothing, but to be cast out, and to be trodden under foot of men." If the salt is pure, it is flavorful and effective. When salt is contaminated with other chemicals or minerals, the taste will be flat and its usefulness is limited. This tasteless salt is only good for keeping grass and weeds from growing in a path.

Without its taste, it fails to fulfill the purpose of flavoring, preserving, melting, or healing.

When I taught elementary science lessons on the five senses, I was always amazed with our sense of taste. God created our tongues to taste only four flavors—sweet, sour, bitter, and salty. It may seem puzzling at first thought but my favorite tastes—chocolate, strawberry, blueberry, mashed potatoes and gravy—are actually smells and not tastes. Our taste buds have nerve endings called gustatory receptors and our nose has olfactory receptors. These specialized nerves work together to give us the joy of tasting.

Let's take a minute to consider these four tastes as they might describe a person. Ask yourself which describes you.

- Sweet—One who is sweet has words full of compassion and grace yet they are strong in truth. They are gracious and sensitive with their responses and comments. They must daily ask the Lord to make them remain true to His Word and be on guard lest their sweetness causes them to compromise or temper truth to not offend instead of speaking the truth in love.
- Sour—A sour person's words and demeanor are full of negative attitudes and spirit. The joy of the Lord is foreign to them. Their negativity clouds all rejoicing and praising the goodness and provision of God. People around them are not interested in what they are saying. In fact, an unbeliever would be quick to say, "If this is Christianity, why would I want to be a Christian?"
- Bitter—Bitterness corrodes a life. Bitterness eats away at the heart of the soul that is full of unforgiveness and resentment. The bitter person sees life through eyes clouded with feelings of false injustice. Pride keeps them from realizing the forbearance and forgiveness of God in their life so they fail to love others as Christ would have them to.
- Salty—Just the right amount of salt makes the taste of something perfect. Too much or too little salt can make the food inedible. So it is with our words. Even words of truth carry a

strong abruptness if not tempered with grace. Words graciously spoken with the balance of genuine love and truth help to open even the coldest of hearts.

LIGHT OF MY WORLD

The Lord Jesus also compares our responsibility to those around us with light. Matthew 5:14*a* says, "Ye are the light of the world." We as Christians are to be a light to a sin-darkened world. For us to have the impact that Christ is referring to, we must be *in the world* to be a light to it. A candle burning in a room with lights on cannot be seen and neither will our impact for Christ be effective if it is only in the midst of Christians. However, you cannot hide a lit candle in a room with the lights off. Even the smallest light dispels the greatest darkness and the greatest darkness cannot extinguish the smallest light. So it is with our light, our witness, in the midst of the lost. The greater the darkness of sin, the greater our witness will be if we boldly live for Him.

Matthew 5:14*b* goes on to say, "A city that is set on an hill cannot be hid." Some would have us believe that we should isolate ourselves and our families from all that is not Christian. This city in Matthew 5 and all its lights are within the sight of others. According to this verse, I must not hide from the world. Like a city on a hill seen for miles around, all that see me observe my testimony, my light.

Is my testimony hidden or easily evident to others? Sinners knew Jesus to be their Friend; He reached out and befriended them! To be Christlike, we too will befriend the lost. Philippians 2:15 declares that we are "in the midst of a crooked and perverse nation among whom [we] shine as lights" if we are letting our light bear His glory. If we each are striving to be that light, we become a collection of lights, a city. Our impact will be even greater. The New Testament name for such a collection of light is the church—a body of saved members who let the light of the gospel shine through them.

LIGHT OF MY HOME

Matthew 5:15 takes this light back to our homes. It states, "Neither do men light a candle, and put it under a bushel, but on a candlestick; and it giveth light unto all that are in the house." We need to fill our homes with the light of our Savior radiating through us. Our family should see our love for the Savior better than anyone else. They see us day after day. We can't fool them. They know us not for our carefully chosen words nor by our action, but by our reactions.

Obviously the most effective place to put a candle is not under a basket or under a bed but on a candleholder where its light will spread across the greatest area. In Luke 8:16 it continues to say, "that they which enter in may see the light." All who enter our home will also see our love for the Lord. The tone, mood, atmosphere of our home will reflect its priorities. How we treat each other also indicates if the Lord is first in our lives or if we live selfishly with unresolved sin. When our family is together on outings, we also reflect our home's love for the Savior. The influence of the wife or mother usually has the greatest impact on the attitudes of the home. If the woman of the house has a walk with the Lord that truly reflects the Light of the World, the Lord Jesus, that home will be a beacon to the neighborhood and community. What kind of light are we in our homes?

LIGHT OF MY ACTIONS

Jesus declared Himself to be the Light of the World in John's gospel. In this passage in Matthew, He is calling us to let our "light so shine before men, that they may see your good works, and glorify your Father which is in heaven." We are to be a reflection of the Lord Jesus just as the moon reflects the light of the sun.

We have nothing within ourselves that can change the lives of others. If we live a life walking closely with the Lord, we will bear His likeness through our obedience and others will see Him. Our actions will be obedient to the Word of God. Our attitudes will reveal the fruits of the Spirit. To make this clear to us, the Holy Spirit directed

Matthew to include a list of actions that require a heart that reflects the Savior. Consider the list of actions from verses 39-44 of Matthew 5.

- Verse 39—" . . . but whosoever shall smite thee on thy right cheek, turn to him the other also."

Reflects patience, longsuffering, forgiving, and forbearing.

- Verse 40—"And if any man will sue thee at the law, and take away thy coat, let him have thy cloak also."

Reflects generosity.

- Verse 41—"And whosoever shall compel thee to go a mile, go with him twain."

Reflects service.

- Verse 42—"Give to him that asketh thee, and from him that would borrow of thee turn not thou away."

Reflects giving.

- Verse 44—". . . Love your enemies,"

"bless them that curse you,"

"do good to them that hate you,"

"and pray for them which despitefully use you, and persecute you."

Reflects love.

Why should we do all these things? What is the purpose of such obedience? Matthew 5:16 clearly declares the answer, "that they may see your good works, and glorify your Father which is in heaven."

LIGHT OF HIS COMPASSION

For salt and light to have optimum impact, they must be from a heart of genuine Christ-like compassion. Throughout the Gospels we see Jesus ministering to the people around Him. Whether He was addressing the masses or sharing truth with an individual, Jesus displayed love. He recognized the true need of the heart and not just the outward symptoms. He met them where they were, and gently but firmly exposed their true need and met that need with Himself. Many times we read that Jesus was "moved with compassion."

How often do those around us move us to empathy and concern? It can make us feel awkward and vulnerable to become too personal with others. Yet, to truly be moved with compassion as Jesus was, we should reach out to those around us. We should meet their needs (1 John 3:17) while pointing them to the Savior for the needs that only He can meet.

As we come to the end of this chapter, I hope you have realized how our fear of people can overshadow our love for the Lord. We probably do not intentionally let others take God's place in our hearts, but too often we fall silent and our love for God takes second place in our hearts. Let's ask the Lord to keep us from glorying in the praise of others and from the denial of the Master by our silence or shallow words. May He make us bold, yet compassionate; make us salt and light so that we may bring Him glory as we love Him more than all others.

GOD'S LOVE DESIRES OUR FRIENDSHIP

John 15:13-15: *Greater love hath no man than this, that a man lay down his life for his friends. Ye are my friends, if ye do whatsoever I command you. Henceforth I call you not servants; for the servant knoweth not what his lord doeth: but I have called you friends; for all things that I have heard of my Father I have made known unto you.*

How marvelous to know that God extends an invitation of loving friendship to each of us. When we have received Him as Savior, He takes us into His precious family. The closer we walk to Him in obedience to His Word, the greater our friendship with Him grows. How truly amazing it is to think that the Creator of this world desires our friendship!

Through faith, we understand that He is who He says He is—*our* Friend! And we are who He says we are—*His* friend! Abraham, in

James 2:23, and the disciples in John 15:13-15 are called friends of God. This friendship is not just a casual acquaintance, but an emotional bonded relationship. God, who is self-sufficient in all things, desires our friendship.

James 2:23: And the scripture was fulfilled which saith, Abraham believed God, and it was imputed unto him for righteousness: and he was called the Friend of God.

Luke 12:15
13-21

CHAPTER 6

More Than Possessions

PACKING AND UNPACKING PUT EVERYTHING into perspective. The joy of unpacking in a new place was dependent upon the discernment implemented at the time of packing. With the careful unwrapping of each box in Wisconsin, my thoughts returned to the last days in South Carolina. The packing of our belongings retraced not only the steps but ultimately the memories of our life as a family.

Where do you begin to put into boxes everything you've accumulated over eleven years? The task seemed unending as I began to sort through our things. Throughout our years in the south, our lives had changed drastically. What had been a necessity those initial years no longer was. When we moved there, all three of our children were still at home. The girls were in high school and Jon was in fifth grade. We had sorted through things when the girls were married and when Jon started high school, but somehow there remained an abundance to remind me of those years.

It was good for me to evaluate and decide what to preserve and what to discard. My heart too often wanted to overrule my logic but reason prevailed. We donated boxfuls to a local ministry to needy people. The objects we had outgrown in one way or another would hopefully meet the needs of another family. A prayer for God to use what He had given us to encourage others accompanied each donation.

We threw away so much! Between the fascinating recycling center and a giant dumpster, our lives became free of clutter and therefore less complicated. The essentials remained. All our worldly possessions filled a myriad of boxes that made the journey north with us.

This process was cleansing in many aspects. We revisited the past years with each thing sorted and packed. Sometimes we laughed; other times we cried. The final conclusion was simple—God had blessed us with amazingly wonderful years as a family. The ultimate lesson was the realization of what really was important. The stuff that surrounded us those years did not make us who we were. It was God's gracious love to each of us that shaped us as individuals and as a family.

I loved the Lord more than anything that I carefully wrapped and boxed. I heard His call to obedience above the clamor of the memories our belongings represented. The call was not easy to answer, but it was right. I thank the Lord for giving me the grace to obey. I was truly striving to love the Lord more than any possession no matter what memories accompanied them.

Luke 12:15: *"And He said unto them, Take heed, and beware of covetousness: for a man's life consisteth not in the abundance of the things which he possesseth."*

Sometimes it's not other people that draw our heart and love from the Lord. You may be successfully keeping the Lord above others in your life. You may be consciously building the right priorities into your relationships, but the things of this world may have captured your heart. Even common things, seeming necessities, may have taken the place of the Lord Jesus in your priorities.

DEMANDS OF THE WORLD

The fascination with the latest technology consumes our society—a society that obsesses over the latest gadget. Devices and the desire to acquire them can become an idol. I have learned to enjoy many of the advances in our world. I have impressed only a few people with my technology knowledge.

I strove to control my temptation to become too familiar with the latest tech in an attempt to remain content. I must admit, however, that there was one new item in recent years that did catch my eye. When

I first learned about it, I was sure as an author and over-all book lover that I would have nothing to do with such a thing. The thought of carrying scores of books on a device small enough to fit in my purse, however, was more than I could resist. My Kindle e-reader goes on every trip with me.

A library in my purse!

The cares of this world are legitimate concerns that can take our attention away from the Lord. We are living in difficult times with an uncertain economy. The reports of improvement offer little hope while the prospect of relief and recovery is still uncertain. Many long for toys and gadgets but are overwhelmed with the demands of the essentials. The advances in technology and the inability to obtain those advances because of financial strain make this a difficult mix.

When our hearts yearn for what we do not have, greed can fill our hearts. Greed is not just the sin of the wealthy; the desire to obtain can consume anyone. Instead of gratitude, our hearts fill with covetousness. What we have or wish we had becomes an idol that takes our thoughts away from God.

How can we keep our love focused on God? Let's consider Jesus' words on this topic. In Luke 12, a man came to Jesus and asked Him to speak to his brother about sharing the family inheritance. The man wanted Jesus to settle the unfair situation. Jesus' response no doubt surprised the man. Jesus clearly stated that He was not a judge or a divider of anyone's family money. He was not going to contribute to anyone's selfishness. Jesus calls us to love Him and love others and not the temporal things of this life.

Jesus continued with a clear warning to "beware of covetousness." With that cautioning, Jesus stated that the key to victory was believing that life is not composed of what or how much we own. True security and confidence is in God alone. Our love must not be for what we possess or wish to possess.

Many people are quick to misquote Paul's inspired instructions in 1 Timothy 6:10. Some say, "Money is the root of all evil." But the verse actually states "the *love* of money is the root of all evil" (emphasis added). That misplaced love brings lapses in faith and many sorrows. The next verses (1 Timothy 6:11-19) give guidelines for how to walk in this world with the proper desires.

We are to follow after:

- Righteousness
- Godliness
- Faith
- Love
- Patience
- Meekness
- Humility
- Sharing
- Generosity

We as Christians have an incredible opportunity. We need to trust God for all our needs while we work hard, but we must never forget that God owns the cattle on a thousand hills. We must remember His promises to supply our need. May we be grateful for all that God has given us!

While we go about the duties of our day, may we be truly content with what God has given to us. Our lives do not consist in the abundance of possessions or in the lack thereof. Thanksgiving for all things should fill our hearts.

Psalm 100:4: *Enter into his gates with thanksgiving, and into his courts with praise: be thankful unto him, and bless his name.*

DEMISE OF POSSESSIONS

In Luke 18:18-30, we meet a rich young ruler who came to Jesus. He was probably a ruler of the synagogue or part of the great council of the nation of Israel chosen for his exceptional character and talent.

This young man outwardly seemed interested in following Christ. In spite of his renown, his life needed more. He needed to evaluate his true love and desire. Let's consider his conversation with Jesus.

RULER'S QUESTION—WHAT MUST I DO?

One day while Jesus taught and preached, a young man came running to Him and knelt at His feet. The young man asked Jesus "Good Master, what good thing shall I do, that I may have eternal life?" (Matthew 19:16). This man was not coming to Jesus in worship, but only out of respect for Jesus as an extraordinary Teacher. He saw Jesus as a righteous man that had discovered the secret to eternal life. Jesus responded, "Why callest thou me good? No one is good but God." Jesus wanted the young man to realize he was speaking to God. This young man no doubt had heard Exodus 34:6 in his religious training: ". . . The LORD God, merciful and gracious, longsuffering, and abundant in goodness and truth."

RULER'S CLAIM—I'VE DONE THAT!

The Lord Jesus knew the young man's true need. Pride ruled his heart and, sadly, he did not realize it. To walk with Jesus, the man would first have to turn from his self-sufficiency. As a ruler in Israel, he was aware of the law. Before sharing that He was the Way to eternal life, Jesus wanted the young man to understand the impossibility of earning merit with God through acts of goodness. Jesus listed five of the Ten Commandments:

- Do not commit adultery.
- Do not kill.
- Do not steal.
- Do not bear false witness.
- Honour thy father and thy mother.

Jesus chose these five for a specific reason. These commandments refer to our relationship with others. The first four commandments about our honoring God and the last one on covetousness, He did not include in this list. The young man no doubt was elated to hear these commands from the Good Master. With great confidence and pride he responded, "All these I have kept from my youth up." Instead of realizing his failure to impeccably keep the law, the young man declared he was eligible for heaven. His good works had paid off. The true state of his heart was hidden beneath the riches and false piety.

I'm amazed at Jesus' response to this young man's smug answer. Many would have shown irritation with such arrogance, but the young man's pride moved Jesus' heart. In Mark 10:21 we read that "Jesus beholding him loved him." In spite of the young man's pride and self-centeredness, Jesus loved him! What a challenge to you and me. How often do we respond with disgust when face-to-face with someone's pride? Jesus countered with love.

RULER'S OPPORTUNITY—COME, FOLLOW ME.

Jesus answered the young man's question about acquiring eternal life. "Yet lackest thou one thing: sell all that thou hast, and distribute unto the poor, and thou shalt have treasure in heaven." Jesus exposed the man's heart issue and clearly told him what he must do. If he wanted eternal life and treasures in heaven, he had to follow Jesus, to love Him supremely, to sell all that he possessed, and to give his money to the poor. As wealthy as this young ruler was, he was spiritually bankrupt and did not even know it.

The Lord Jesus gave this man an incredible opportunity. Jesus extended an invitation. "Come and follow me." Jesus was asking him to leave all the world had to offer and walk with Him. Can you imagine? Wouldn't that be amazing to walk for just five minutes of this life beside the Son of God? Yet, this young man looked at Jesus and said, "I won't." He loved himself and his wealth more than he loved his neighbors or God.

RULER'S FAILURE—I'M SORRY, BUT I WON'T!

The issue was not the young man's money. Jesus isn't against people rich in the things of this world. Money and possessions were this young man's priority. Genuine faith would have led this man to surrender all he had to the Lord. He would have done whatever the Lord asked of him. Jesus' request was simple—love God more than these! This young man was face to face with the Son of God, but his love for his riches was such an obstacle that he walked away in unbelief. It wasn't that he couldn't follow Christ; he simply wouldn't.

What a sad story! I want to challenge you to evaluate your own heart. Could it be possessions or the cares of this world have taken God's place in your life? Jesus said it is easier for a camel to go through the eye of a needle than it is for a person rich in the things of this world to accept Christ. Their self-sufficiency and pride kept them from seeing their need of a Provider. Whether you own a little or a lot, what God has given to us is to be used for His glory! When we love Christ above all, the things of this world are meaningless.

DELIGHT OF THE DISCIPLES

The desire for riches hinders many from coming to Christ. Many people's hearts are tied very closely to the things of this world. Maybe if the ruler owned few earthly possessions, like the disciples, it would have been easier to give it away. His riches influenced his thoughts and deeds. That influence kept him from receiving the most valuable thing a man can possess—a relationship with God.

The disciples were observing the whole exchange between Jesus and this young ruler. If this man who had everything couldn't be a disciple, what hope did they have of continuing with the Lord? They had nothing to offer. Jesus turned to His disciples and carried the meaning of this exchange to its fullest extent.

DISCIPLES' QUESTION—WHO THEN CAN BE SAVED?

In Matthew 18:26, the disciples ask, "Who then can be saved?" The disciples assumed that riches were indicative of God's blessing and favor. They knew they had nothing compared to this rich young man. If this one with great acclaim could not be saved, what hope did they have? Their hearts were fearful that all their devotion and effort was in vain. Don't we often think the same? We look at those with more than we have and think if we only had what they have, it would be so much easier to love and serve the Lord.

Do you ever thank the Lord for what you don't have? How many of us are convinced that if we had just a little more our lives would be much easier? We even try to piously say we could serve the Lord better if we didn't have to be concerned about making ends meet! We instead should be grateful for whatever God has given us—little or much—and use it for God's glory.

Jesus explained that it is difficult for a rich person to receive His gift of salvation. When we surrender our hearts in obedience to the Master, He changes our love from the riches of this world to a love for Him.

DISCIPLES' STANDING—THEY HAD ALREADY FOLLOWED!

The lesson of this scene comes first from Peter. In Luke 18:28, Peter declares, "Lo, we have left all, and followed thee."

In classic Peter style, Peter boasts of all he and his friends left to follow Christ. Peter's words may have magnified their surrender, but they truly had left all. Jesus acknowledged that the disciples had already done what this rich young ruler refused to do. They had embarked on the life of faith with Christ. The Apostles had left their homes, their occupations, and their families. They had already left all and followed Jesus. He looked at these dear friends and assured them that they knew the joy of His love, His goodness, His grace, and His eternal care—things this rich young ruler would never know loving his possessions more than Christ. Jesus brought the disciples focus back to reality and off the young ruler's earthly riches that they lacked.

Jesus ended this important lesson with a precious promise. All who love Him more than the possessions of this world will receive manifold more. All who surrender possessions, family, houses, etc. will be blessed many times over in this life and in eternity.

> Luke 18:29-30: *And he said unto them, Verily I say unto you, There is no man that hath left house, or parents, or brethren, or wife, or children, for the kingdom of God's sake, Who shall not receive manifold more in this present time, and in the world to come life everlasting.*

We should not be focused on accumulating earthly treasures. Our life does not consist in the abundance or in the lack of things in this world. When we love Christ above all, we will hold things loosely. We will share what we have with those in need. We will use whatever possessions and riches we have to minister to those around us.

Consider the following summaries of these verses. God's Word teaches us what loving God more than our wealth and possessions will look like.

> 1 John 3:17-18: *But whoso hath this world's good, and seeth his brother have need, and shutteth up his bowels of compassion from him, how dwelleth the love of God in him? My little children, let us not love in word, neither in tongue; but in deed and in truth.*

If we see a brother or sister in need, we will do whatever we can! By those gestures of love we show the love of God within us.

> Luke 3:11: *He answereth and saith unto them, He that hath two coats, let him impart to him that hath none; and he that hath meat, let him do likewise.*

John the Baptist taught his followers that if they had two coats, they should share with someone in need. If they had food, they should share it with those who hungered.

> James 2:14-17: *What doth it profit, my brethren, though a man say he hath faith, and have not works? can faith save him? If a*

> *brother or sister be naked, and destitute of daily food, And one of you say unto them, Depart in peace, be ye warmed and filled; notwithstanding ye give them not those things which are needful to the body; what doth it profit? Even so faith, if it hath not works, is dead, being alone.*

Our deeds demonstrate our love for those around us. Our words alone are worthless—empty words will not warm or feed anyone.

> Matthew 25:35-40: *For I was an hungred, and ye gave me meat: I was thirsty, and ye gave me drink: I was a stranger, and ye took me in: Naked, and ye clothed me: I was sick, and ye visited me: I was in prison, and ye came unto me. Then shall the righteous answer him, saying, Lord, when saw we thee an hungred, and fed the? or naked, and clothed thee? Or when saw we thee sick, or in prison, and came unto thee? And the King shall answer and say unto them, Verily I say unto you, Inasmuch as ye have done it unto one of the least of these my brethren, ye have done it unto me.*

When we feed the hungry, give drink to the thirsty, and clothe the naked, it is as if we've done it for the Lord Jesus Himself. If we refuse to provide for the least of these, it's as if we have refused to do them for the Lord Jesus.

When we love Christ above all, our perspective is eternal. Our greatest desire will be to lay up treasures in heaven, not riches here on earth. We will realize that the glories of heaven far outweigh what we lack in this life. May we daily strive to be rich in the true riches of God's economy!

GOD'S LOVE IN ACTION

Throughout Jesus' earthly ministry, He was moved with compassion for the people around Him. Compassion is a love that recognizes a need and responds to meet that need. Compassion is a love that acts! In Psalm 86:15, tells us that God is a God full of compassion.

> Psalm 86:15: *But thou, O Lord, art a God full of compassion, and gracious, longsuffering, and plenteous in mercy and truth.*

Although crowds of people followed Jesus, He saw each individual and their specific needs. Jesus responded with love to each one. To the blind, He gave sight. To the lame, He gave strength and movement. To the hungry, He provided food. To the sick, He restored their health. To the grieving, He brought comfort. To the troubled, He shared peace. Whatever the need, He responded with an act of love that healed!

Matthew 5:43-44: *Ye have heard that it hath been said, Thou shalt love thy neighbour, and hate thine enemy. But I say unto you, Love your enemies, bless them that curse you, do good to them that hate you, and pray for them which despitefully use you, and persecute you.*

In Matthew 5:43-44, Jesus challenged the disciples to have compassion not only for those they love but also for their enemies. Friends and family are easy to love and show compassion for. Jesus wants our compassion to be a reflection of His.

Romans 5:8: *But God commendeth his love toward us, in that, while we were yet sinners, Christ died for us.*

Jesus' greatest act of loving compassion was in giving His life on the cross. There He took the place of all mankind. Only He, God the Son, could take upon Himself the sin of mankind and pay in full the debt that man owed. His glorious resurrection confirms that God the Father accepted Jesus' loving, compassionate sacrifice for all mankind.

CHAPTER 7

More Than Myself

HOLIDAYS WERE HIGHLIGHTS OF OUR year. The simple traditions were welcomed events as the seasons passed. By the time our years in South Carolina were drawing to a close, our children could carry out the festivities with little need for Mom's directions. Their knowledge didn't keep me out of the action, however. The plans would easily flow from beginning to end.

Our favorite celebrations were Thanksgiving and Christmas. For me the special dinners were the highlight. My daughters and I would work side-by-side in our tiny kitchen with amazingly coordinated precision.

The instruction began when they were little girls. Standing on a chair beside me or perching on the countertop just out of reach, they watched and helped until those recipes were as familiar as a storybook.

What a mess the kitchen would be! But what fun we had. Now years later, we worked like a team. Oh, the recipes had changed through the years, but the overall holiday meal was a masterpiece.

When I faced the first Thanksgiving in Wisconsin, I felt an emptiness that I had been afraid would accompany this special holiday without our family. A family from church graciously invited us to share the day with them, but it was not the same. That Thanksgiving included other monumental events of which I would not be a part. Our oldest daughter was about to give birth to their second little girl. My mind was constantly drifting to the thought of this little bundle's arrival without me there. I had seen our first two granddaughters within minutes of their births. Now I was a thousand miles away from the hospital, and this new little girl would arrive any minute. I had planned to go in a couple weeks to help but that did not seem quite the same. (She did indeed arrive Monday of Thanksgiving week and I wasn't there.)

Our second daughter's little girl would celebrate her second birthday the Friday after Thanksgiving. We had been together for her first birthday the past year. But that year she would open our gift without us there. We would miss the look on her face as she pulled the paper off unless they took the picture at just the right moment. My heart was sad to think I'd have to experience this celebration with pictures only or maybe a video to document a few minutes of the party. It just would not be the same.

We were scattered. Did the traditions and memories of our world for nearly thirty years have to be scattered too? It was all because we were in Wisconsin.

When I took my pitiful heart to the Lord, He again reminded me of the question He asked Peter that morning by the seashore. Did I love Him more than these? This time His question did not involve my love for my children. This time it was my love for myself. The emptiness of my heart caused by miles of separation had made me discontent with my current state. My self-pity allowed those hundreds of miles to draw my heart away from the Lord Jesus. I loved myself more than I loved my Master who had called me to serve Him.

My heart was grieving because of a loss of closeness to my children. Instead of indulging in my selfish thoughts, I needed to turn my gaze upon the One I serve. He is the God of comfort. He would give grace to match my need. To resent the distance put my concern for myself above my love for God. I had become my own idol. I needed to say with the Apostle John, "He must increase, but I must decrease" (John 3:30).

Sometimes we focus only on ourselves and forget there are people around us that God wants us to minister to and love.

How do we take care of ourselves and still be able to help other people? There are mothers, grandmothers, and daughters reading this that are exhausted from caring for others. You are approaching a limit that will leave you ineffective. When you take the time to have a cup of coffee, read a book, or take a leisurely walk, you feel guilty.

In the midst of our caring for the people around us, we can become weary. Our personal, emotional, and spiritual strength diminishes if we minister to others without refreshing our own heart. We will feel empty and weak. The truths from God's Word that should encourage our hearts seem lost in the confusion of our weary soul. We need to stop and sit at the feet of the Savior.

Time with the Lord refreshes our priorities and renews our focus. Our service to others becomes a joy and not a resented obligation. If we love God supremely, we will serve those around us as if we were caring for the Lord Jesus Himself.

In John 13, Jesus ministered to His disciples and gave us a beautiful picture of how He wants us to serve others. Jesus had just finished the Passover meal and knew that His betrayal and death were soon to come. Looking from face to face, the memories of their years together were close to His heart. He loved these men—"loved them unto the end" (John 13:1). His thoughts were turned to the glories of heaven that He would soon be returning to with redemption's plan complete.

How appropriate it would have been for Jesus to rise from the table and ask the men to bow before Him in worship. He was worthy of such a demand. Instead of asking for the homage He deserved, He "laid aside his garments; and took a towel, and girded himself. After that he poureth water into a basin, and began to wash the disciples' feet, and to wipe them with the towel wherewith he was girded" (John 13:4-5).

Jesus, the second Person of the Godhead, carried out the task usually assigned to the lowliest servant of the house. Jesus' humility and selflessness is our example to follow. Our love for Him should reflect His sacrificial love for us.

Philippians 2:7-8 states that Jesus "made himself of no reputation, and took upon him the form of a servant, and was made in the likeness of men: And being found in fashion as a man, he humbled himself, and became obedient unto death, even the death of the cross."

Does your love for God bring you to this kind of selfless service for His glory? Are you following His example in your service to others? In Matthew 16:24-26, we see the Lord Jesus' call to discipleship. Jesus gave these words specifically to the disciples who had been His companions and students in the days of His earthly ministry. His message was simple but life-changing when obeyed. Jesus was calling them to deny themselves, take up their cross, and follow Him.

> Matthew 16:24-26: *Then said Jesus unto his disciples, If any man will come after me, let him deny himself, and take up his cross, and follow me. For whosoever will save his life shall lose it: and whosoever will lose his life for my sake shall find it. For what is a man profited, if he shall gain the whole world, and lose his own soul? or what shall a man give in exchange for his soul?*

BELIEVER'S CALL—DENY HIMSELF

Before Jesus addressed the need for the disciples to deny themselves, Jesus laid an important foundation. He told the disciples that He would go to Jerusalem and suffer many things from the elders, chief priests, and scribes. This suffering would lead to His death; but in three days, He would rise from the dead.

Peter immediately rebuked the Lord Jesus. "Be it far from thee: this shall not be unto Thee" (Matthew 16:22). He didn't want Jesus to die. A few verses earlier, Peter had declared Jesus to be the Messiah. Rather than recognizing the Messianic fulfillment of Jesus' words, Peter interpreted them within the context of the immediate. The Lord Jesus quickly stopped Peter's offensive words.

With the explanation of the coming events and the rebuke of Peter's perspective, the disciples were now ready to hear the Savior's call. If they were to follow the example of the Lord Jesus, they needed to completely deny themselves by realizing they were not their own.

The word *deny* means to not think about yourself and your preferences and interests but give yourself wholly to Christ and share in His shame and death. This same word was used when Peter denied the Lord the night of Jesus' arrest. Peter swore he didn't know the Lord Jesus. His words, "I know not the man" (Matthew 26:74) were piercing when referring to the One who had done so much for him. Denial was a cruel response.

Yet, this is what the Lord was asking His followers to do. The Lord Jesus was calling them to set aside their earthly desires and to unconditionally surrender to Him.

Only by God's grace, His enabling power, can we forsake ourselves. What blessing awaits those who come to such a place!

BELIEVER'S SURRENDER—TAKE UP YOUR CROSS

The second step in this process of loving God more than ourselves, is to "take up our cross." As I studied the meaning of these words, I found my imagination stirred by two opposites. First, to take up your cross would not to be impatiently dragging it along behind you.

Trying to move my son's book bag comes to my mind. The minutes between high school and ball practice or work would often be few. He would be gone sometimes before I would realize that his book bag full of textbooks remained by the back door. To move the backpack was no small task. I had learned that I should not even try to lift it. So I would simply drag it to a safer location.

My attitude was a mix of impatience and reality—impatience that I had to move it and the reality of my weakness.

I noticed through the years that many Christians dragged their cross in a similar fashion. They appeared irritated and inconvenienced that God would ask them to live the Christian life. Their cross was an unwelcomed burden at best.

Other Christians kept their crosses hidden from the view of all but a few, in case they might be held accountable to walk the Christian life. This approach kept them open to options that would satisfy their desires. After all, if the right opportunity arose, they couldn't risk losing it to maintain a testimony. If conviction did cross their path, it could be easily retrieved to pacify their conscience.

Obviously neither of those approaches to cross-bearing was what Jesus had in mind. If His words were to "take up your cross," that would rule out dragging it behind or hiding it in a pocket. If we obey the plan that Jesus intended, we'll better understand what cross-bearing is all about.

TAKE UP

To *take up* is to pick up, lift it high and carry it. This definition declares that we, as disciples, are to lift our cross high to be seen by all. We need to daily crucify ourselves by yielding to all that God instructs us in His Word.

Some have been quick to call only the burdens of this life their cross. They claim financial hardship, difficult people, or physical disease is their cross to bear. Don't our unsaved neighbors and co-workers struggle with these same issues? Carrying our cross means to stand with Christ in the denial, dishonor, hardships, and agony that He endured.

No doubt some of the common issues of life are complicated by our relationship with the Lord; but to take up our cross is to be ready to pay any price for Christ's sake. It is a willingness to suffer in this life and, if necessary, become a martyr for Christ's glory. Revelations 12:11 states it this way: ". . . they loved not their lives unto the death."

Luke 9:23: *And he said to them all, If any man will come after me, let him deny himself, and take up his cross daily, and follow me.*

In Luke 9:23, we learn that we are to lift up our cross daily if we desire to follow Christ as we should. This surrender is not a onetime event in our lives like our salvation, but a daily dying to self. How quickly our selfish hearts can usurp the place of authority that we should reserve for the Lord. Throughout the course of a single day, we may have to take up our cross again and again as we surrender our self-centered hearts to Him.

Luke 14:27: *And whosoever doth not bear his cross, and come after me, cannot be my disciple.*

2 Corinthians 4:10-11: *Always bearing about in the body the dying of the Lord Jesus, that the life also of Jesus might be made manifest in our body. For we which live are alway delivered unto death for Jesus' sake, that the life also of Jesus might be made manifest in our mortal flesh.*

This verse in Luke 14 clarifies the meaning of a true disciple of the Lord Jesus to be one who bears his cross no matter what it entails. We endure with joy the persecutions and trials that may come because we follow the Master. To bear the name of Christ-follower or disciple, we must moment-by-moment set self aside and identify with Him; in identifying with Him, we reflect Him; in reflecting Him, others will see God and His working in and through us.

HIS CROSS

If we are called to take up our cross, it is imperative that we understand what it means when it refers to "his cross." A cross has come to be just a casual part of our lives. We see crosses on jewelry as well as hanging on walls in a variety of decorative patterns. The salvation and victory that the cross represents has not always been what people thought of first. The cross was the cruelest, most shameful form of capital punishment used by the Romans on the worst of the empire's enemies. Historians believe they crucified about 30,000 people during Jesus' earthly life.[1] People could easily picture a condemned person walking along a road carrying part of his cross.

Throughout the centuries many have wanted the blessings of the Christian life without a willingness to carry such a cross. At the first sign of suffering, they abandon the Savior. A Christian that loves the Lord Jesus more than all else runs to the cross and willingly lifts it daily to walk in His footsteps. Because of all that the cross represents, we as disciples must live at the foot of the cross surrendered to God. Galatians 5:24 clearly explains, "They that are Christ's have crucified the flesh with the affections and lusts."

If we are to take up our cross, we are going to have to unreservedly surrender to God. Whatever our abilities, strengths, and weakness, we give them to Him. Denying ourselves completely. Full and complete surrender to Him. When a woman denies herself and takes up her cross, only then is she prepared to follow Jesus as He desires.

"MUST JESUS BEAR THE CROSS ALONE"

Must Jesus bear the cross alone,

And all the world go free?

No, there's a cross for everyone,

And there's a cross for me.

How happy are the saints above,

Who once went sorrowing here!

But now they taste unmingled love,

And joy without a tear.

The consecrated cross I'll bear

Til death shall set me free;

And then go home my crown to wear,

For there's a crown for me.

by Thomas Shepherd[2]

BELIEVER'S MISSION—FOLLOW HIM

Jesus called Peter, Andrew, James, and John from their fishing nets. He said, "Come, and I will make you fishers of men," and they came. He saw Matthew sitting and collecting taxes. When He called to Matthew to come, he came. I don't know why, but many have the idea that if they surrender to the Lord's call on their life it means straight to Africa and a mud hut.

There is no in-between. They think that if they don't hang on tight to the things of this world, they are doomed to the tarantulas and snakes. Dear friend, your greatest joy is found being exactly who God made you to be. Do you realize God made you perfect to accomplish His will for your life? Doing what He has called you to do and being what He wants you to be brings genuine delight. Full surrender should accompany every moment of our lives. Can you say, "I love you, Lord, so much that I give you all of me?"

Jesus described this surrendering as "following" and gave this mission to all who trust in Him as Savior. To *follow* means to walk in the footsteps of someone who has gone before, to become a disciple of that person, and to hold to their beliefs. 1 Peter 2:21 declares that ". . . Christ also suffered for us, leaving us an example, that ye should follow his steps." The Lord Jesus desires that we walk as He walked, with our actions, our words, and our thoughts following His lead. Without the knowledge of Him that we gain through the pages of His Word, it is impossible to follow.

Those who love themselves more than the Lord Jesus don't follow Him. Their misplaced love leads them down a path that is far different. The Bible gives us some clear examples of common excuses that men use for following their agendas. Let's look at a few of these examples in Luke 9:57-62.

HOUSING SECURITY

Verses 57-58: "And it came to pass, that, as they went in the way, a certain man said unto him, Lord, I will follow thee whithersoever thou goest. And Jesus said unto him, Foxes have holes, and birds of the air have nests; but the Son of man hath not where to lay his head."

INHERITANCE (FINANCIAL) SECURITY

Verses 59-60: "And he said unto another, Follow me. But he said, Lord, suffer me first to go and bury my father. Jesus said unto him, Let the dead bury their dead: but go thou and preach the kingdom of God."

FAMILY/FRIENDS SECURITY

Verses 61-62: "And another also said, Lord, I will follow thee; but let me first go bid them farewell, which are at home at my house. And Jesus said unto him, No man, having put his hand to the plough, and looking back, is fit for the kingdom of God."

Jesus' final words to these excuses were, "Don't look back!" When God calls us to follow Him, our focus should be obedience and the ultimate display of our love. No lesser matter should take precedence over God's work, if we want to be used by God. Every Christian must decide daily whether or not to love Christ above all else, to take up his cross, and to follow Christ.

This cross lifting is not an easy thing. No wonder our hearts hurt. It's not usually easy to do right and sacrifice; but it is right! Let's ask the Lord to give us the grace to walk with joy in spite of any circumstance. May we offer Him a sacrifice of joy continually. May we lift our crosses high and follow the Lord today.

Can you say, "I love you, Lord, so much that I surrender all of me?"

Our move to Wisconsin made me evaluate my application of these truths.

May I deny myself—Put God FIRST in my every thought and action.

Take up my cross—Leave my family to serve the Lord in Wisconsin.

Daily—Not just a one-time surrender, I must deny self and pick up my cross everyday!

Follow Me—Move . . . to Plymouth, Wisconsin! May I lose my life in You, Lord, and in Your service.

A variety of responses met our plans to move to Wisconsin. To those who were in full-time ministry, the news was a blessing. They understood the calling of the Lord and gave us precious encouragement. Their excitement all but matched ours. Many expressed their love for us and that they would indeed miss us, but they were thrilled that we were headed back into the service our heart had never fully left.

From those who taught at the science center with me, the responses were mixed. Some were excited but many, as I mentioned in a previous chapter, were somewhat confused. Why would we leave our children and granddaughters? With a church on every corner of this southern city, why couldn't we just find a church in town to hire my husband? To leave our family that we were so close to made no sense to them.

I understood completely the variety of opinions that we received. The perspective depended on the understanding of cross bearing. Those who had lifted their cross and followed understood. Those who had no idea what discipleship was all about were puzzled. I found encouragement from those who understood and opportunity to share God's Word with those to whom this truth was unknown. The move was unfounded apart from God's will. The move was not optional to remain obedient to His will.

Academically, I had it settled. In my heart, I still had times of struggle. My memories went with me across the miles; but the loneliness was often extremely real. Without the knowledge of this cross bearing, I don't think I could have adjusted as quickly as I did. I knew the Lord understood better than anyone else. He comforted my sad heart and still continues to. He showed me ways to use technology created just for a grandma to keep in touch with her grandchildren and children. Since that first Thanksgiving, He allowed us scores of holidays to share at one house or another. He gave His love and grace to fill the emptiness that I felt.

I can think of other times in my life that the Lord has asked me to carry my cross. Some of those times were easier than others to lift my cross high. This cross is the heaviest I've had to carry. No, the world will never understand. I believe God does.

He knew what was best for my granddaughters and me. I find it hard to admit that it's best for us to be a thousand miles apart. But I trust God to be God. If I love God more than myself, I will continue to obey His call to lift my cross up and follow Him. What's your cross? How high are you lifting it?

GOD'S LOVE IS INCOMPREHENSIBLE

The rapid development of technology is staggering. In just a short time information multiplies; advances in every area plunge forward making it nearly impossible for the average person to stay current. The growth of information resembles an explosion. A person does well to follow just one area. We can try to keep pace, but it becomes virtually impossible. Regardless of what we may be able to grasp in this life, understanding God's love is beyond human understanding at its best.

Ephesians 3:19: *And to know the love of Christ, which passeth knowledge, that ye might be filled with all the fulness of God.*

God's love surpasses our human reasoning, experience, and knowledge. Only as we trust Christ as Savior can we catch a glimpse of His sacrificial love. When we accept His work on our behalf, we realize the vastness of His magnificent love.

The greatest demonstration of His love is the cross. God desires us to be filled with His abundance. Filled to the top with His greatness and glory. Filled and overflowing with His unsurpassed love.

The songwriter, Isaac Watts, pictured this beautifully in the following words:

WHEN I SURVEY THE WONDROUS CROSS

When I survey the wondrous cross

On which the Prince of glory died,

My richest gain I count but loss,
And pour contempt on all my pride.

Forbid it Lord, that I should boast,
Save in the death of Christ, my God;
All the vain things that charm me most—
I sacrifice them to His blood.

See, from His head, His hands, His feet,
Sorrow and love flow mingled down;
Did e'er such love and sorrow meet,
Or thorns compose so rich a crown?

Were the whole realm of nature mine,
That were a present far too small:
Love so amazing, so divine,
Demands my soul, my life, my all.[3]

CHAPTER 8

More Than My Fears From Without

THE FAMILIAR IS SAFE. EVEN if it may not have all the pleasantries we desire, the commonplace gives us confidence. My world in South Carolina was familiar. It had become my home. Growing up as a pastor's daughter I had lived in several states. To "go back home" didn't mean anything to me. Each place I had lived had done God's work to mold me into what He wanted me to be, but then we moved on. So after a few years living in South Carolina, Greenville became my "back home". Although I knew God would one day return us to full time ministry, I was grateful for a place I could consider my hometown.

My move to Wisconsin took away that familiar. The removal of the known left my heart somewhat fearful. I had to get acquainted with all new people, town, countryside, climate, lifestyle, and more. I had made these kinds of adjustments many times before, but my past did not eliminate the present. The fearful uncertainty of the new replaced the old.

2 Timothy 1:7: *For God hath not given us the spirit of fear; but of power, and of love, and of a sound mind.*

Much in this world causes even the bravest of us to fear. On any given day, frightening scenarios occur around every corner. Our world is full of unrest and uncertainty. The stability of one nation rests on the economy of another. The rioting and protests seem to call people of all ages to unite. The problems facing our nation are unprecedented.

The path to recovery is uncertain with citizens becoming further and further divided.

The crisis doesn't end when you turn off the evening news or put down the newspaper. The silencing of the outside noise only accentuates the conflict within many homes. Family fears relate to the physical, financial, and spiritual burdens that wreak havoc to their home. In spite of all the technology to communicate faster and easier, conversations seem minimized to a few random words forming an impersonal message. When trials overwhelm, few seem to have the time or wisdom to face them with confidence in God.

God's Word tells us how we can be free from fear. 2 Timothy 1:7 declares that God has not given us this spirit of fear. His gifts of power, love and a sound mind will only occupy a heart that gives those fears to Him. This freedom is not the absence of problems or trials but a peace in the midst of the trial. That peace comes from a relationship with God and confidence in God.

Perhaps you have never thought about something negative becoming your greatest love. When our thoughts focus more on our problem than on God, that problem has become our idol. In spite of words of loyalty to the Master, our primary focus can leave the Savior and our fears can occupy our heart and mind. When our fears hold our thoughts enslaved, they seize our love for God.

If we compare God to our fears, we soon realize that no fear is greater than God. How well do you know God? Too often we fail to trust Him as we should because we are ignorant of His power. While teaching a series on faith to the ladies in one of my Bible studies, my study led to three statements about God and our responsibility to Him.

These biblical statements, I believe, form a significant part of the foundation of our faith. Our walk with the Lord should be guided by these life-changing truths. Since God is greater than all our fears, our love and faith are secure in Him. When we live by these three principles, God will exchange our fears for a steadfast trust.

1: God is. I must strive to know Him better.

> Philippians 3:10: *That I may know him, and the power of his resurrection, and the fellowship of his sufferings, being made conformable unto his death.*

Our knowledge of God is vital for securely trusting and for quietly resting in Him. We must be in the Word daily, diligently striving to know Him better. Our knowledge of Him must always be growing. We learn about His character as He declares who He is through the pages of His Word.

We will find that He is love, joy, peace. He is the great I Am. He is Faithful, Comforter, Creator, and Lord. In His sovereignty, He is forgiving, gracious, gentle, holy, and righteous. The endless list becomes more magnificent when we remember that He is unchanging. The pages of Scripture portray Him as He was then and still is today. He is the only thing in our life that is the same yesterday, today, and forever. No matter the chaos in the world around us, we can confidently say, "God is."

No matter what burden we face, we should be well acquainted with the One who can solve any need and carry any burden. We need to strive to learn of Him not just for ourselves but for those around us who face the hopelessness and fearfulness of a life without God. Our thoughts should instantly turn to the Savior as we walk through each day. We often forget that we are in a spiritual battle. Satan seeks to destroy us and those we love. With a daily time in the Word reinforcing and growing our knowledge of God, we find the strength to stand and resist Satan's attacks. When our entire world seems devastated, we can be confident that God is. We must strive to know Him better!

2: God can. I must trust Him without reservation.

> Psalm 40:5: *Many, O LORD my God, are thy wonderful works which thou hast done, and thy thoughts which are to us-ward: they cannot*

be reckoned up in order unto thee: if I would declare and speak of
them, they are more than can be numbered.

When we learn who God is, we realize that God deserves our complete trust. Through His working in the lives of the people in the Bible, we begin to grasp the magnitude of God. When we realize that He is unchanging, we will desire to trust Him without reservation. Because He loves us with a perfect love, we can trust Him to send into our lives only what is needed to make us more like Him. Even when He sends trials, we can trust Him. He sustains us, grows us, builds us, and matures us through whatever means He sees best.

He never sends us more than we need. With each trial He sends assurance, strength, comfort, wisdom, healing, grace, and whatever else we need to bring about His desired end for us. We are so limited with what we can imagine God doing. He can do the impossible! Nothing is beyond His power and control!

We see God's power and provision all throughout His Word. He reveals to us that He can do what is necessary to accomplish His perfect plan. The God of the Bible is our great God. As Esther, Mary, Hannah, and scores of other Bible women trusted God, so should we. He can do today what He did centuries ago for people of faith. May we walk in the confidence that this truth should give us—God can. We must trust Him without reservation.

The bridge between "God can" and the next step, "God will," is the knowledge that God can do all things for us. We do not question His power or character, but we sometimes question His love. We recognize His goodness and power; but we don't believe He loves us enough to display it for us personally. What good news it is to realize that God not only is Who He is and can do what His Word declares, but He *will* do it for you and me. Because of His great love, we who are so unworthy can know His power in our hearts and lives. That marvelous fact leads us then to truth number three.

3: God will. I must rest in His unfailing promises.

> Jeremiah 33:3: *Call unto me, and I will answer thee, and show thee great and mighty things, which thou knowest not.*

We need to believe that God will!

It is not enough for us to have a knowledge of God and His working within the pages of His Word. We must realize that the promises of His Word are for us. Who He declares Himself to be is exactly Who He wants to be for us. The powerful promises He decrees are promises for us to claim. His promises are not empty words, but unfailing pledges given to all who call Him Lord. When we understand Who He is, what He can do, and what He will do, we cannot help but rest in Him.

How many times do we miss the blessing of seeing God work because we fail to rest in His promises? We assume He needs our help in solving the circumstances of the moment. We worry and fret until we arrive at a plan that we can carry out without relying on God to show Himself strong.

Jeremiah 33:3 says, "Call unto me, and I *will* answer thee, and show thee great and mighty things, which thou knowest not" (emphasis added). This verse clearly commands us to call on God and undeniably promises that He will not only hear but will answer in a great and mighty way.

Too often our first response to God may be, "Why? Why me? Why now?" We focus on explanations and not on the promises. If we believe that God will be true to His Word and will answer us when we bring our needs before Him, we will focus on the promises and not need the explanations. Are you resting in the promises of God's Word? When we love God more than our fears, we rest confidently in His working. That confidence frees us to accept God's answers and methods.

We must be in the Word to know God's promises. Sometimes people expect God to do what he never promised to do. Let's consider an example to help clarify. God has the power to heal any disease, but God does not promise to always heal. However, God definitely promises

His grace (2 Corinthians 12:9), His comfort (2 Corinthians 1:3-5), and His presence (Deuteronomy 31:6), 1 Chronicles 28:20, Hebrews 13:5) in times of sickness and even death. We can rest in His promises no matter the circumstances.

These three truths must be our foundation. We need to see every page of God's Word teaching us who God is, what God can do, and what God will do. We need to rest in these truths and share them with others through our words and actions. This, dear friend, is the hope that people around us need. When dark days come, these truths will sustain us. When fear and uncertainty overwhelm us, our loved ones, and our neighbors, these truths will meet the need. Why? God alone is the answer to all our fears. In light of these truths, let's consider some common fears.

THE FEAR OF AUTHORITY'S DEMANDS
DANIEL 3—SHADRACH, MESHACH, AND ABEDNEGO

The Babylonians took Shadrach, Meshach and Abednego captive. Their story of courage is familiar even to the youngest Sunday school child. Their fear could have easily overtaken their love for God, but instead they remained true to God. They had followed Daniel's lead and remained faithful in spite of the many miles that separated them from their homeland and families. Because of their fearless stand for God, He put them in positions of leadership; but in Daniel 3, they faced a difficult decision. Nebuchadnezzar erected an idol that represented his authority and position. When the musical instruments played, all the people were to bow in worship of this idol and the king it represented. The penalty for refusing was death in a fiery furnace.

These three Hebrew men faced a life-threatening choice. They could obey the king and live or remain true to God and die. Their love for God far exceeded their fear of dying. When the instruments played, all of Babylon bowed before the image except for Shadrach, Meshach, and Abednego. They refused to bow. These young men realized that their obedience to God was their priority no matter the consequences. Jealous peers quickly carried the news of the young men's refusal to Nebuchadnezzar. The king was livid. How dare these men whom he had placed in positions of authority not bow to his image! The king demanded the three be brought to him immediately. Surely, he could persuade them to obey his command when they recognized his resoluteness.

After repeating the command to the three Hebrew men, Nebuchadnezzar saw no change. They assured him that their refusal was not a casual preference. Much prayer had given them the courage to face the punishment. Their prayer was not to convince God to do things their way. Their hearts had sought God's will. They would bow to no one but the God of heaven. The king's anger flared. "Who is that God that shall deliver you out of my hand?" (Daniel 3:15).

"If it be *so*, our God whom we serve is able to deliver us from the burning fiery furnace, and he will deliver us out of thine hand, O king" (Daniel 3:17). The words must have stung the heart of this proud king.

The men were unshaken. They firmly believed that their God was able to deliver. They knew Him as the faithful, omnipresent, omniscient, and omnipotent God. God in His power would give them the courage, faith, and sound mind to walk into the fire unafraid.

As these young men faced this king, they understood the king's power and authority. He had signed into law their outcome. He was bound to do what he declared. These three men boldly proclaimed that even if God choose not to rescue them, they still would not bow. God would provide the grace to face the furnace. These courageous men had already learned that God gives grace to walk the path that He chooses for us. In His wisdom, God asked them to trust Him and accept the outcome. He might not choose to deliver; but their obedience to God would glorify His name.

Job 13:15 states the heart of these brave men. "Though He slay me, yet will I trust in Him." Although the government does demand our obedience in certain areas, we do not have a king that is threatening death if we do not worship as he desires. We may fear government's demands and directions, but our freedom exceeds most other countries around the world. We all, however, have authority of some kind over us—husband, employer, pastor, laws. Sometimes that authority can be cruel, harsh or untrustworthy. God, however, can be trusted and obeyed.

These young men faced the dilemma of obeying the authority over them or obeying the Lord. After diligent thought, they believed that God was able to deliver them. Although they didn't know how He would do it, they were confident that God would show His power.

Daniel 3:18 takes their faith to another level. "But if not" identified their faith, their trust in God. Whatever answer God gave, they were ready to accept it. They truly believed that God's will was best. Shadrach, Meshach, and Abednego were submitting to the will of God without reservation.

Many of us would have prayed for the easy solution—skipping the fire completely. We must be willing to trust God without hesitation. Even if it means suffering, we must be willing to accept God's plan. Christians are suffering for the name of Christ all around the world. In the United States, we know nothing of that type of persecution. Some of our greatest concerns are our personal comforts—the temperature of the church auditorium, the length of the service, the comfort of the pews.

People in many places meet in secrecy with a constant threat of persecution; yet the persecuted church flourishes. Through even the worst treatment or conditions, God wants to teach us, grow us for His name to be honored.

Shadrach, Meshach, and Abednego was determined to do right whether God delivered them or not. The king ordered the furnace heated seven times the normal temperature.

The men throwing them in the furnace died from the intense heat. In verse 25, King Nebuchadnezzar looked into the furnace and saw the unexpected. Four men were loose and walking in the midst of the fire. This wicked king declared the fourth Man to look like the Son of God.

Rather than the three Hebrew men dying in the fire, they had fellowship with this heavenly Messenger. This wicked king recognized and acknowledged that only a God unfamiliar to him could do such a thing. He recognized God's power (Daniel 3:29). Only the true and living God could do something so amazing.

The willingness of these three men to stand for God was greater than their fear of the fire or the king. God honored their love by sparing them. The fear of the furnace didn't overtake their love for God. God received the glory in this king's life and kingdom. The news of God's glory went throughout the country. All the people heard the story as Nebuchadnezzar declared to the entire nation the power and glory of the Hebrew God. The decision to love God more than fear of the demands of authority affected a whole nation.

When lonely, fatigued, or overwhelmed, our fears need to be set aside. We have a God that is greater than all. When we love Him most, the impact is significant.

FEAR OF FAMILY'S OPINION
1 SAMUEL 17:28—DAVID AND HIS BROTHER

Have you ever noticed how the words of those we love tend to hurt us more than the comments of acquaintances or strangers? Those we love most can wound us with the briefest of statements. They seem to know where we are vulnerable and do not hesitate to strike our most tender spots. Just the thought of such an encounter can make even the confident scrutinize their words. Fear can mount when a family member's opinion differs from our own. David faced such fear when he brought the food to his brothers in the battle against the Philistines and their champion, Goliath.

Eliab's harsh words greeted David when he entered the camp. "Why camest thou down hither? I know thy pride, and the naughtiness of thine heart; for thou art come down that thou mightiest see the battle."

David had had to leave the sheep to bring the food to his brothers in the midst of the battle. Eliab implied that David neglected his responsibilities at home. Eliab felt David unworthy of any task but watching the sheep and accused David of being too proud to remain focused on the shepherding. Eliab accused David of only wanting to follow in his older brother's footsteps and be a soldier only to gratify his vanity and ambition. David's curiosity, he said, was secondary only to his vain desires for fame as a soldier. Eliab's entire accusation was false and opposite of David's true heart.

Opposition from family can be a great hindrance to a genuine desire to walk with God. This false attack by his older brother could have kept David from being where God could use him to defeat Goliath and go on to rule Israel. How often do we allow the opinions of those closest to us draw our heart away from the Savior? We fear these important people more than we love the Lord when we let their words change our course.

David loved God more than he feared the words of his brother. When faced with the harsh words of Eliab, David remained steadfast. David focused on who God was. David remembered what God could do. And David rested in what God would do.

To David, God was . . . .

- The Living God
- The Lord of Hosts
- The God of Israel
- The God who saves
- The God of the battle
- The God of deliverance

To David, God could . . .

- Defeat the enemy
- Deliver us from the enemy
- Prepare us for what lies ahead

- Use our experience to grow us to greater service
- Use our pain to help others
- Save with or without sword and spear

To David, God would . . .

- Work with a strong arm. He will display His strength, power and give the victory.
- Build us, grow us, stretch us.
- Display His faithfulness.
- Not be defied. Goliath's demands and mockery of David's God did not go unchecked.

Because of his faithfulness to God, David jeopardized the relationship between his brother and him. When you love God most, as David did, you realize that your relationship to God is far more important than any relationship here on earth. As much as David wanted the respect of Eliab, he wanted the approval of his heavenly Father more, no matter the consequences. David obeyed God and faced what seemed like an undefeatable enemy. He saw God use him to deliver Israel in a remarkable way. David showed great courage when he didn't allow the opinions of an older brother stop him from seeking God's plan and obeying it.

FEAR OF THE ENEMY'S THREAT
1 SAMUEL 17—DAVID AND GOLIATH

The cause is not always certain, but trials arrive like an unexpected enemy of our soul. Unbelievable situations without easy or swift solutions often replace a peaceful life. Of all the challenges none is as great as dealing with pride. The actions of others reveal the arrogance of the enemies' heart, but our response reveals that pride is also alive and well within our own hearts.

Throughout God's Word, we meet heroes of the faith that faced a variety of enemies. Their enemies were unlike ours, but they were just as real. Circumstances were vastly different, but the courage and faith with which they faced their enemies reveal their love and confidence in God. No enemy could surpass the greatness of their God and none of our fears are more powerful or greater than God.

We allow these enemies to become idols when we dwell on them without the ability to overcome them.

David was one of the heroes from God's Word that fearlessly faced his enemy. One of David's enemies was Goliath—a formidable giant that daily challenged the armies of Israel. It was not uncommon for two nations to settle their battles with two warriors fighting each other. The outcome of the two would determine the fate of the whole army.

In 1 Samuel 17, David approached the army camp. He immediately observed the fear the Israelite army had for the giant. In fact, this whole army was terrified of the one giant and that terror overpowered their trust in God. When Goliath taunted the army of God, Israel's soldiers cowered.

David knew that he could not face the enemy's threats in his own strength. David had seen God's deliverance when faced by a lion and a bear on the hillsides as he tended his sheep. He faced Goliath in God's strength, which was far greater than the strength of the lion, the bear, or a nine-foot giant. All the earth would know that there is a God in heaven, a God in Israel.

The victories over the enemies of our day will also come if we are resting in the strength of the Lord. When you and I love God most, we will love Him more than we fear others. The only way we will defeat the enemies of our lives will be in God's power. We may acknowledge this power with confident assent, but are we living as if we believed it? The only way that we will ignore the attacks of our enemies and defeat them will be in God's strength.

We help our children not be afraid of things by telling them that God is watching over them; they have no need to fear. Do we apply that truth to our lives?

Dangers and problems will still arise, but we do not have to face those threats alone. When our giant trials come, God is with us. He does not ask us to fight alone, but He does ask us to trust in Him alone.

David faced Goliath with just a slingshot, some smooth stones, and a cause that lifted the name of God. David accomplished what God intended. Our all-powerful God will accomplish what He intends in every trial we face. Attacks will come, but He goes with us. Let Him lead and sustain. He will give the victory.

Let's look at the truths from God's Word.

I must love God more than I fear my enemies. If I think more about my enemies than I think about God, I've allowed my enemies to take the throne of my heart. I must bring my thoughts back into captivity. I must love God with my every thought. With my focus on Him, my enemies' influence fades.

I must live each moment with these truths as the guiding force behind all I do, say, and think—God is. God can. God will. Not only is God greater than all my enemies and fears, He alone can defeat them or use them in my life for His glory. He loves me so much that He will work on my behalf. Therefore I must know Him, trust Him, and rest in Him. He will accomplish His will for me.

I cannot do His necessary work in the life of someone else. I must let God be God. He knows all and can do all. I've no need to fear or worry. God is sovereign. My enemies are His to deal with. I must love Him more than those I fear and rest in Him.

GOD'S LOVE CASTS OUT OUR EVERY FEAR

1 John 4:18: *There is no fear in love; but perfect love casteth out fear: because fear hath torment. He that feareth is not made perfect in love.*

Many times in the course of a lifetime, we can be overcome with fear. When we are resting in the love of God, we have no need to fear. God loves us with a complete and perfect love. We do not need or want anything else because His love is sufficient. The Lord Jesus wants us to cast out our fear. That means we need to let go of whatever causes us to fear and walk away with our eyes fixed on Him.

Our fear is replaced with peace when we trust and rest in His power. Even in the midst of difficult days, we can rest in His strength and presence to overshadow us because He loves us.

Isaiah 43:2-4a: *When thou passest through the waters, I will be with thee; and through the rivers, they shall not overflow thee: when thou walkest through the fire, thou shalt not be burned; neither shall the flame kindle upon thee. For I am the Lord thy God, the Holy One of Israel, thy Saviour: . . . Since thou wast precious in my sight, thou hast been honourable, and I have loved thee.*

CHAPTER 9

More Than My Fear of Circumstances

THE SOUTH QUICKLY TURNS A person into a Southerner.

Although my husband and I grew up in the north, our almost twelve years in South Carolina had turned us into Southerners. We welcomed the thought of four distinct seasons that Wisconsin would give us. We were excited to think that the heat and humidity that accompanied our lives those past years would soon be replaced with colder winters, but also by more enjoyable temperatures of summer.

With Christmas just a few weeks before our big move, it was the perfect time to prepare for our new climate. We unwrapped all the necessities—boots, gloves, hats, and parkas. Little did we know that our new attire would quickly reveal our new resident status. Our tourist-like wardrobe would soon give a chuckle to the seasoned northerners we were about to invade.

When the day to move arrived, two men from the Wisconsin church flew down to drive the moving truck for us. What a thoughtful plan. That meant we could say our good-byes to our daughter and her family in South Carolina, and then drive to our other daughter's home in Tennessee to spend a couple days with them before heading to our new home.

When the day came to begin our journey, the winter weather greeted us long before we had expected it. Traveling to Wisconsin meant we had to endure the worst winter storm to hit Kentucky.

Kentucky? Who knew Kentucky would present such a challenge. Wasn't Kentucky a southern state?

For the next few days, snow and ice covered the beautiful rolling countryside. We traveled only 230 miles in one eight hour day. At one point, we had to stop for over three hours. Our plan to arrive in Plymouth had to be changed. Another night in a motel was needed to wait for the roads to be cleared.

The conditions of the roads brought reality into perspective. We were moving to a new world if we could survive the drive to get there.

Our arrival was extra sweet after such a grueling trip. The snow piles lined the streets of our new town. No snow was falling at the moment, but the bitter cold temperatures greeted us. Our ability to adapt to this new white-covered world was going to be put to the test. When we opened the garage door, there sat the biggest snow blower we had ever seen—a gift from our new church family. We somehow knew at that moment we could adjust. Between our new wardrobe and this wonderful machine, we could face these circumstances without fear.

Joshua 1:9: *Have not I commanded thee? Be strong and of a good courage; be not afraid, neither be thou dismayed: for the LORD thy God is with thee whithersoever thou goest.*

There are many circumstances in life that are beyond our control. In spite of our detailed organizing and planning, life brings us many unexpected, unstoppable, unalterable events. The actions and decisions of others can change the course of our lives at a moment's notice. Our helplessness can be overwhelming. Sometimes the issues at hand seem to devour us as they take control of our world. Fear invades without warning when these circumstances surround us. Fear consumes and leaves us anxious and afraid.

Unless we surrender our fearfulness to the Lord, it will draw our focus off the Savior by consuming our thoughts. The circumstances intended to draw us closer to the Master will attempt to capture the throne of our heart.

The disciples faced many trials as they followed God's plan for establishing the church. The book of Acts shares many incidents that tested the love of the Apostles. Were they going to love the Lord most or were they going to capitulate to the demands of their circumstances?

CIRCUMSTANCES' POWER—ACTS 4:13-ACTS 5:32

In Acts 4:13-31, the disciples asked God to show Himself strong in the midst of the persecution they faced. They prayed for God to work in and through them and to grant them courage to live for His glory and preach the gospel. Peter and John were commanded by the authorities to stop preaching and teaching in the name of Jesus. They bravely responded, " . . . we cannot but speak the things which we have seen and heard . . . And now, Lord, behold their threatening: and grant unto thy servants, that with all boldness they may speak thy word" (Acts 4:20, 28-29). God answered their prayer and with great confidence, they continued to share the truth.

In Acts 5, the apostles unrelentingly preached the message of the risen Savior. God used the apostles to do signs and wonders and to heal multitudes of sick people in Jerusalem and the surrounding area. Many were saved and added to the growing number of believers. The excitement and growth of the people filled the High Priest and the other religious leaders with indignation. The Jewish leaders arrested and imprisoned the apostles. During that night an angel of the Lord opened the prison doors and sent the apostles back into the temple to continue preaching the message of the risen Savior.

When the officers came to the prison where God's men had been, they were amazed to find the guards and doors in place, but the men were no longer there. The news soon reached the religious leaders that the apostles again were preaching and teaching in the temple. The captain and officers went to the temple, and without violence brought the apostles back to appear before the high priest and his council.

The questioning began with, " . . . Did not we straitly command you that ye should not teach in this name? and, behold, ye have filled Jerusalem with your doctrine, and intend to bring this man's blood upon us" (Acts 5:28).

In spite of their fear of severe punishment, the disciples immediately were willing to be obedient even in a public venue. Their love for God was greater than their fear of the government's vicious threats.

The Apostles were beaten again and commanded to not speak in the name of Jesus. Instead of cowering to the demands of the religious elite, they praised God for counting them worthy to suffer for His name's sake. They did not stop sharing the news of the Lord Jesus in the temple and in every house. Their love for God far exceeded their fear of the religious leaders' threats.

If just released from prison for sharing your faith, would you immediately share it again in a public place? I am afraid I would have gone somewhere secure, private, and hidden away! God asks very few to suffer for His name; but God does ask that our witness go beyond the occasional moments of organized soul-winning or visitation. Our witness is our daily activities and conversations. Our life needs to proclaim what we believe. Although it is not easy to live with this degree of love, by God's grace, we can live His message before others, as we love Him more than we fear our circumstances.

CIRCUMSTANCES' DARKNESS—ACTS 16:12-40

All writers probably have times that seem to be their best moments to write. For some it may be mornings, bright and early before the rising of the sun. For me that would never work. My best sleep is the few hours preceding the ringing of the alarm or my husband's rousing me awake from the final details of my last dream of the night. For me to get up early to write would not be productive.

My best time to write is at night. For a number of years, sleep has not come quickly. I have the burdensome mindset that all the events of the day need reviewed, and my plans for the next day orchestrated precisely before I'm ready to fall asleep. By the time I analyze the memories and appraise the upcoming day, I am often more awake than when I went to bed. At times like this I find writing to be my best method of finding slumber.

To write from my heart is easier at night. The house is quiet, but the night sounds have taken over. I have no idea what creature I hear singing his nocturnal serenade, but his voice is distant, steady, and calming. The lack of noise is almost startling in comparison to the bustle of our busy days. In the stillness, one can analyze straightforwardly the cares of the day without interruptions. Without the contemplation of night, many directions from my Lord would be lost.

With the previously mentioned policy instituted a number of years ago, I do not waste sleeplessness. I determined that if sleep refuses to come, I would use the time seek my Savior's face. Through reading His Word or trusted books that teach me of Him, I have learned the joy of turning the seemingly endless night into a time of precious fellowship, learning, and writing.

How true this is of the "night" times in our lives. I have seen the Lord take the circumstances of my life that seemed the darkest and quietest to teach me the most of who He is. The lessons seem to be deeper, better learned because they came when all other avenues of apparent deliverance had come and gone.

Oh, that I would praise Him for the dark nights of my life! Why do I continue to resist such times of learning? Why do I desire it to all be over instead of resting in the arms of my Savior? Will He not carry me through? It is in the darkness that I can most vividly see that He is my Light and my Salvation. Thank You, Lord, for the nighttime.

How easy it is, however, to lose sight of the benefit of dark times. When the events of our lives seem to only bring more uncertainty, darkness can become the lens through which we see everything. The darkness can distract us and draw our focus off the Savior's love for us and our love for Him. Instead of praising Him, we allow our thoughts to lead us down a dark path of uncertainty and pain. Before we realize it, our circumstances become an idol and our love for the Lord wanes.

At such trying times, it is essential that we see our circumstances through the eyes of faith. I believe that the foundation of our faith statements that we discussed in chapter eight give us the key to loving God even in the darkest times. In this age of texting, I decided that my *God is, God can, God will* steps of faith needed to be even more concise to remember and apply the truths easily.

God is. Know Him.

God can. Trust Him.

God will. Rest in Him.

These brief statements help us remember these truths. If we are basing our lives on a foundation of faith, we will continue to love God as we should. When grim circumstances bring devastation into our lives, these statements give us hope and focus.

In Acts 16, Paul and Silas faced a very dark and difficult trial. For preaching about the Lord Jesus, the leaders of the city shackled these godly men and placed them in prison. Most of us have no idea what such an experience would be like, but we all know the fear of desperate times. Our times of deep trials can bring us great fear and perhaps a glimpse of the bondage that Paul and Silas experienced in this passage. Our love for God can be shadowed by the bleakness of the situation. Paul and Silas teach us a valuable lesson by their response to this seemingly hopeless night.

Paul and Silas were in Philippi, a major city in Macedonia that was the crossroads for travel between Europe and Asia. On the Sabbath, they went out of the city and met a group of women praying by the riverside. One of the women, Lydia, believed and became Paul's first convert in Europe.

When they travelled throughout the city, a girl possessed with an evil spirit called out, "These men are the servants of the most high God, which shew unto us the way of salvation." After many days of her interruptions, Paul commanded the evil spirit to come out of her. The men who used her as a source of income became angry and took Paul and Silas to the magistrates. The men charged Paul and Silas with teaching customs that were not lawful for the Philippians to hear or practice.

Immediately the magistrates attacked Paul and Silas, beat them, and cast them into prison. The jailer, fearing for his own life, placed them in the inner prison in stocks to be sure they could not escape.

In the midst of this horrible place and concealed by the shadows of the night, Paul and Silas sang praises to God. Although alone and forsaken in this gloomy prison, the words of their songs revealed their hearts. God was with them and He would receive their praise no matter the circumstances. Their songs carried throughout much of the prison. They were unseen but not unheard.

We often forget that our responses communicate a loud message. Our words may be few but even the tone of our voice reveals the attitude of our heart. Because of worry and lack of trust, our words may be a hindrance to others who need to hear the Gospel message. We forget that other people can hear us. Although our acquaintances cannot see our heart, our words reveal it.

An earthquake interrupted Paul and Silas's songs. The foundations of the prison shook. Bands fell off. The freeing of the prisoners terrified the jailer who knew he would bear the penalty for the prisoners escaping.

Paul and Silas stopped the jailer from taking his life. The jailer called for a light to guide his steps into Paul and Silas' prison cell. He desperately needed the answer to his questions, "Sirs, what must I do to be saved?" Paul and Silas responded, "Believe on the Lord Jesus Christ, and thou shalt be saved and thy house." Not only did the jailer believe, but so did his family as the men of God spoke "the word of the Lord to all that were in his house" (Acts 16:32).

Paul and Silas were able to see heaven in the midst of the dungeon. Together Paul and Silas sang praises to God in the midst of their darkness, pain, and suffering.

These men of God are an example for us. When there is no hope and no apparent relief in sight, we can still see heaven. At times the circumstances of our lives are painful, and hopelessness crushes like darkness. That darkness surrounds us and causes us to either cry out in great pain or to rejoice in our great God.

Our love for God should exceed our fear. Even in the darkest of night, God loves and cares for us. Desperate situations can distract us from trusting and worshiping God as He desires. Paul and Silas focused on heaven. May we see beyond the circumstances of the moment and praise God continually. May our fear never exceed our love for God.

God gives to us as parents or teachers special verses that minister to the hearts of the little ones in our care. When I think back over the years that my children were growing up, I immediately think of a verse that ministered to my heart as well as my children's.

Psalm 56:3: *What time I am afraid, I will trust in thee.*

These ten little words gave comfort and solace on many a scary night or fearful adventure. The psalmist no doubt knew the fear that nighttime can bring. Guarding his sheep on the Judean countryside, the threats to his flock could have struck fear in the heart of the young shepherd. The dangers were real, but the loving shepherd's heart reassured his flock of his continual care and protection.

With this picture in my mind, I often calmed the childhood fears of my little ones. God could be trusted. God was there and would take their fears and exchange them for His reassuring love and strength. There was no need to fear because the Lord Jesus was near to watch over them.

Many times throughout the years, my children remembered this verse and applied it once again as they faced fearful days. For example, when our older daughter was in fifth grade she wrote a play for her class to perform. The story was of a father that was called to war—a relevant theme to her classmates and her. The play told the story of a little boy who was fearful of his dad being gone. His mother reassured him with truths from God's Word. The verse Jenny had incorporated into the story was Psalm 56:3. My heart was touched as I heard this verse become the solution to the play's conflict. How wonderful it was to see it remained a part of her heart as she used it to reassure the story's fear-filled character.

When we love God more than all else, our confidence will be in Him alone. I heard a young father beautifully explain this verse, Psalm 56:3, to his daughter. When we trust God, it is like we are holding onto His hand. When fears come, we feel we cannot hold on to keep our grip secure. When our grasp becomes impossible to maintain and we let go, God is still hanging onto us. When fear overcomes our hearts, He will not let us fall. The fear of our circumstances should never take our focus from loving God like He deserves. No matter the circumstances, may we trust God and love Him above all else.

GOD'S LOVE REJOICES IN HIS CREATION

Zephaniah 3:17: *The Lord thy God in the midst of thee is mighty, he will save, he will rejoice over thee with joy; He will rest in His love, He will joy over thee with singing.*

God enjoys His creation. Zephaniah declared that God, in fact, rejoices over His children with great joy that is expressed with singing. When God looked at His creation in the early chapters of Genesis, He announced that it was very good. His love for His creation includes each one of us.

The phrase, "He will rest in His love," means that He will quiet us in His love. What a precious thought! When we are struggling with the fears of this world, He wants us to go to Him, our Creator, for comfort and consolation through His matchless love.

Psalm 104:31: *The glory of the Lord shall endure for ever: the Lord shall rejoice in his works.*

We learn that the Lord rejoices in the work of His hands. He hates the sin that corrupted His perfect world, but He delights in the lives that seek to do His will. In fact, He responds in genuine affection to

His children that delight to bring Him glory through their obedience and worship.

May we, by God's grace, trust Him even in the darkest of days. May our love and confidence in God far exceed all of our fears.

CHAPTER 10

More Than the Fear of the Unknown

THE LAST FOUR YEARS THAT we lived in South Carolina, I was the dental educator for the health department of Roper Mountain Science Center. Roper Mountain was an incredible complex dedicated to educating children and their families from our county and the surrounding area. The children would visit the center for school fieldtrips or summer science day camps. I loved being a part of this phenomenal place. Learning was fun and exciting. I saw hundreds of early elementary children every week.

By the time the children would reach second grade, they were familiar with my presentation on brushing and flossing. In spite of the five and a half foot wide mouth and six-foot toothbrush, after three years of visiting me, they knew what I was going to tell them (even if they weren't practicing it). To keep these knowledgeable attendees attentive, I re-wrote my program to include a pretend trip to the dentist. I would begin their lesson with the question, "Are you too old to pretend?"

Delightful squeals of "No" were the normal responses.

Before the presentation was over, we would have the whole dental office crew. I would choose children from the audience to join me on the stage and dress them to depict a patient, hygienist, and dentist. I emphasized the jobs of each person in the midst of delighted laughter over their classmates' new oversized attire. The key to the program's success was pretending. The students would miss the fun of the program without using their imagination.

What happens to our ability to pretend as we get older? Some never lose their ability to create and imagine. Most of us are still pretenders and children delight when we share our creativity. However, the passing years have proven that some things we imagine actually become realities. These unwelcome occurrences make us more fearful of passing thoughts. Our fears are no longer simple but complicated by the experiences of life.

The older we grow and the more people come into our lives, the greater our fear of the unknown becomes. Those of us with children and grandchildren look at this world and fear can easily overtake us. What will life be like for our little ones by the time they are adults? Fearful unknowns have replaced our creative imaginations. With our imaginations unchecked, we can become afraid without reason. Instead of thinking on "whatsoever things are true" (Philippians 4:8), we develop a "great fear where no fear was" (Psalm 53:5).

Has our fear of the unknown replaced our confidence in God and dampened our love for Him?

ABRAHAM'S JOURNEY

Many well-known Bible characters teach us how to face the unknown. God called Abraham to leave everything and to go to an unknown place. Hebrews 11:8 states, "By faith Abraham, when he was called to go out into a place which he should after receive for an inheritance, obeyed; and he went out, not knowing whither he went." This moment of life-changing obedience placed Abraham in this list of people with great faith.

How amazing Abraham's obedience was. I can only imagine Sarah's response when Abraham announced that they were moving away from Ur of the Chaldees. She no doubt attempted to remain calm and seek the facts with an open mind.

"Where are we moving, Abraham? When are we moving? How long will it take us to get there? What do you know about the place we are going? What are the people there like?" she may have asked.

With Abraham's answer of "I don't know" to each of her questions, Sarah's voice probably became more strained and frantic. To move is difficult enough. To move with no information, would have escalated the panic already generated in Sarah's heart. Poor Abraham. To say yes to God was easier than not being able to answer Sarah's inquiries. His lack of answers to these reasonable questions could have shaken his confidence in God. Abraham, however, remained obedient and proceeded to orchestrate this relocation.

God did not give Abraham a compass or map to follow. As this man of God set out in obedience, he could not consult the stars to guide his path since God had given him no specific path to follow. Abraham faithfully followed God's direction one step at a time. With each step, he drew closer to the Promised Land and to greater fellowship with God. With that greater fellowship came a greater love for God. The fear of the unknown was not great enough to keep Abraham from obeying God's call to the new land. Any fear that may have been there gradually diminished as God's faithfulness was confirmed repeatedly.

Instead of the stability that they may have anticipated in this new land, there were new, unknown factors to face. When Abraham and Sarah finally arrived at their designated destination, God did not direct them to establish a permanent residence. Their home remained a tent not unlike the one they had used as they traveled these thousands of miles from Ur to Canaan. According to Hebrews 11:9, "By faith he sojourned in the land of promise, as in a strange country, dwelling in tabernacles with Isaac and Jacob, the heirs with him of the same promise."

Abraham never had a permanent dwelling the rest of his life.

"He permanently lived in temporary housing!" a pastor friend said as he referred to Abraham's living status in a sermon on this passage.

Our house in South Carolina was similar temporary housing. No doubt Abraham's dwelling was a greater inconvenience than mine was; however, we never would have chosen that house to live in for over eleven years. The bedrooms were perfect for our children's high school and college years. Although this little house served us well, I could not unpack. For all those years our garage remained half full of containers. It was not until we were in Wisconsin over a year that I was finally able to empty those boxes. For all those years in South Carolina, we considered it a temporary house as we waited for God to open a door to ministry.

God's promises were abundant to Abraham. God covenanted with Abraham to make him a father of many nations. Over a quarter of a century before giving Abraham and Sarah their son, Isaac, God promised that their descendants would number as the stars in the heavens and the sand on the seashores. God pledged that all the land that Abraham could see in any direction would be his.

Abraham confidently accepted these promises that God had made him; but he never saw all of them fulfilled (Hebrews 13:11).

Although Abraham lived with many unanswered questions and unfulfilled promises, he walked with great confidence in God. Abraham's love for God was greater than his concern for the unfulfilled promises. Abraham demonstrated his love and trust by his obedience to God when the unknown dominated his world. When we question God's care, we need to remember that He knows all things! We, too, will face uncertainties; yet, we can rest confidently in our great God. We may not see the answers to our prayers in our lifetime, but our obedience should reflect our confidence in God. The unknown is secure in the hand of the Almighty.

NOAH'S MISSION

Rain is just a part of our everyday lives. Either the need for it or the abundance of it makes rain the topic of many casual conversations. If you live in a dry climate, the dryness is a daily reminder of the lack of rain. If you live where rain showers are a part of everyday life, your umbrella is never outside your reach.

I remembered vividly the reality of unexpected rain when I attended college. In the Midwest, weathermen forecasted rain and we prepared; but, I quickly learned that the possibility of a downpour in the South was forever looming. One afternoon a deluge caught me totally off guard. I was on the way to the library and then to meet David, who was my boyfriend at the time, for a soda before going to dinner. I was nearing the library when one of the infamous, unexpected rain storms arrived.

Although I was on a covered sidewalk, the combination of rain and wind completely drenched me. Within seconds I looked like I had just stepped out of the shower. With my library visit and soda date postponed, I headed back to the dormitory to get presentable once again. Although I survived, my favorite coat shrunk proving its "Dry Clean Only" label was a wise warning.

With rain so common, it is difficult to imagine a life without it. God introduced rain in judgment of great wickedness. In Genesis chapter six, we learn that God was grieved at the wickedness in the hearts of men. "And God saw that the wickedness of man *was* great in the earth, and *that* every imagination of the thoughts of his heart *was* only evil continually" (Genesis 6:5). God declared that He would destroy all living things. Genesis 7:4 says, "For yet seven days, and I will cause it to rain upon the earth forty days and forty nights; and every living substance that I have made will I destroy from off the face of the earth."

In the midst of this wickedness, there was a man that lived with a sincere love for and obedience to God. The Bible declares that Noah was a man that walked with God. God directed Noah to save himself, his family, and the living creatures from the flood that He would soon send to judge the people's wickedness.

The unknown filled God's instructions to Noah. God's plan would succeed only if Noah obeyed His directives to the minutest detail in spite of the lack of information. Hebrews 11:7 states that, "By faith Noah, being warned of God of things not seen as yet, moved with fear, prepared an ark to the saving of his house; by the which he condemned the world, and became heir of the righteousness which is by faith."

For the next 120 years, Noah prepared the ark so he, his family, and the animals would survive the flood that God would send. Noah faithfully obeyed the Lord building this giant boat to be ready for the unheard of thing called rain. I can only imagine the ridicule that Noah must have received from his neighbors and friends. When he tried to explain, his words only confused the mockers; no one knew what Noah was talking about.

How was Noah to gather the animals? How would he possibly capture and contain all the animals that were to be on the ark? God sent the animals and gave Noah the wisdom to fill the ark as He intended. Noah seemingly never doubted the instructions of God; he obeyed God when surrounded and perhaps overwhelmed with the unknown. His neighbors' endless questions and his elusive answers did not deter Noah.

No matter what others thought, Noah's family believed him. They were willing to walk with Noah as he walked with God. They may have seen his moments of doubt, but they would have remembered his obedience when after a full year they finally stepped off the ark into a new world. The unknown did not overcome Noah's love for God. Noah remained fearless in the midst of the fearful unknown.

MOSES' LIFE

A third Bible character that clearly portrayed a fearless love for God was Moses. When we read the account of his life in Exodus or the summary of it in Hebrews 11, we soon realize that his life was full of the unknown. Believing that God had a special plan for Moses' life, his mother hid him for three months to spare his life from Pharaoh's commandment to kill all baby boys.

Can you imagine keeping a baby quiet for three months? She loved God more than she feared the decrees of an ungodly king. The unknown outcome was worth the risks that it demanded.

When the baby's cries and squeals could be hidden no longer, Moses' mother prepared a little basket of bulrushes. With every weave of the basket and every spot that she daubed with slime and pitch, this young mother would have prayed that God would protect her baby boy from the unknown dangers while he floated on the Nile.

Even with his sister's watchful eye, Moses could have faced death from this precarious position. The crocodiles waited for the next little boy to be thrown to them. His unknown destiny would be in the hands of his rescuer. It was Pharaoh's daughter that retrieved his little basket from the bulrushes, and her decision for Moses' future was unchangeable.

Moses' life of uncertainty continued when he fled the penalty of killing an Egyptian, watched a bush burn without it being consumed, and listened to the call of God to deliver His people from slavery. Every time he faced Pharaoh to demand the release of God's people, Moses did not know what Pharaoh's response would be. When he led the children of Israel out of Egypt, Moses was responsible for the provisions for nearly two million people. Moses loved God more than he feared all these incredible situations. He continued to trust God and obey.

When Moses stood at the bank of the Red Sea, he faced the impossible. How was he to lead this chosen nation safely to the Promised Land? The Egyptians were behind them, the mountains on each side of them, and this vast Sea in front of them. It was totally unknown to this new leader how God would deliver them.

Exodus 14:13: *And Moses said unto the people, Fear ye not, stand still, and see the salvation of the LORD, which he will shew to you to day: for the Egyptians whom ye have seen to day, Ye shall see them again no more for ever.*

God's response to Moses was, " . . . Fear ye not, stand still and see the salvation of the Lord" (Exodus 14:13). In this case, Moses was to do absolutely nothing to obey God.

Busyness can conceal fear and make us feel and look productive. In His obedience, Moses showed his love for God by once again waiting on God to bring the deliverance. Moses no doubt was afraid of what lay ahead, but he boldly proclaimed God's words and led them in obedience. Moses left us an example of how to love God more than fearing the unknown. His obedience demonstrated a fearless love for God. However great the fear of the unknown may be, love for God should overrule.

Many other examples of Bible people illustrate this fear. No fear is more powerful than our God! We must live like we believe it. What is unknown to us is simply a part of the plan of God.

When the January day came to load the truck and move to Wisconsin, I was grateful for the help that the Lord sent me. No matter how diligently one prepares there are still dozens of things left to be boxed and cleaning to do. The Wisconsin church sent down two men to help us load, and then drive the truck north for us. We appreciated their coming to help. My husband drove to the airport to pick them up as I continued the last minute packing.

My husband recounted his thoughts on the way to the airport. The reality of what we were about to do all but overwhelmed him. The magnitude of the unknown that lay ahead of us engulfed him.

What exactly was he doing? Wisconsin? Why was he making such a drastic change for our family? What would the distance do to all of us? His thoughts were flooded with doubts that refused to be suppressed.

The men stopped for dinner at a Cracker Barrel Restaurant before starting back to our home. The typical decorations at the restaurant were geared to welcome weary travelers. While contemplating the dilemma in his heart his eyes fell on a plaque hanging on the wall.

Jeremiah 29:11: *For I know the thoughts that I think toward you, saith the* Lord, *thoughts of peace, and not of evil, to give you an expected end.*

The words were a balm to his anxious heart. There was no need to fear the unfamiliar, the unknown. Our Lord had everything in place;

He knew what lay ahead. His desire was to bring us peace and not evil. He had a hope and a future planned for us. We could confidently rest in Him.

GOD'S LOVE IS IMMENSE

In Ephesians 3, Paul prayed for the believers to comprehend the love of God. He knew they would need to know and understand God's love for them to stay focused and growing. Without this understanding, they would overestimate their love for God and others. The descriptions of His love that Paul gives help us know the love He desires for us to reflect.

Ephesians 3:17-18: *That Christ may dwell in your hearts by faith; that ye, being rooted and grounded in love, May be able to comprehend with all saints what is the breadth, and length, and depth, and height.*

According to Ephesians 3:18, we cannot measure the breadth, length, depth, or height of God's love for us. His love is as immense as His character. His love is unable to be measured by any standard. His hundreds of names express the greatness and eternality of His character and power. If we were to consider each name or characteristic of God, we would also see the magnitude of His love reflected. Here are just a few of His names that show the greatness of His love.

- Jehovah Adonai (Self-existent)—His love has no beginning.
- El-Olam (Eternal)—His love has no ending or limit.
- El-Elyon (Immense)—His love is awesome in majesty and supremely exalted.
- El-Shaddai (All-sufficient)—His love is all we need.
- Jehovah-Rophe (Healer)—His love heals our every wound.[1]

What a great God we serve. What a great love He shares!

CHAPTER 11

More Than My Past and Present

SOMETIMES IT'S EASY TO LOSE sight of the influence and impact we have on those around us. Our daily routines overshadow the lives we touch until we are oblivious to the souls that we come in contact with. Even ministry can consume our thoughts, and we forget the lives that we are affecting.

Our pastor had insisted there be a reception to send us on our way to Wisconsin from South Carolina. The date was set and arrangements made. After the evening service of our last Sunday in town, we would have the opportunity to tell our church family good-bye.

The night before the reception we said farewell to our son who flew to Spain to attend an university there that semester. Dave and I had stayed in a motel near Atlanta, and our heads were still swimming with emotion when we arrived home. We had just enough time to change and attend our last service with these dear people who had become our second family.

Pastor called us to the platform and publicly thanked us for all we had done throughout the years, and then invited everyone to a time of fellowship after the service. For the next couple of hours, Dave and I talked with the unbelievable number of people that waited through the receiving line to talk to us. We were overwhelmed with the kind words and precious memories shared with us. Little did we realize the impact we had had on so many individuals in a variety of ways. Their stories were from their hearts. The emotion of their words matched the walk of their lives. These dear people had been our students, our children-in-the-Lord, and our friends.

Our church family had helped us pray for the right door to open for full-time ministry. Now God had given us all the answer to that prayer. We had never thought about Wisconsin being that place of His will, but in just a few days, we would be on our way. For this night, however, it was the past that we rejoiced in as our friends shared their memories and gratitude as well as their fears and concerns.

We had challenged them through the years to look to Jesus, the only One who could meet all their daily needs. We now prayed that God could use the truths we had tried to faithfully share as the foundation for countless blessings in the days ahead.

God was calling us on to minister to others. Many would help us finish packing and load our truck that week, but this night was our farewell. Although we loved these people and our ministries to them, we loved the Lord more. We must obey His leading.

The events of yesterday often shape our current life and ministries. Some circumstances of our past we would rather forget. Past decisions can look foolish from today's perspective. We also have highlights in our life that are still a source of encouragement and accomplishment. We all have positive and negative experiences to recall, but God doesn't want us living in the past or focusing on it instead of Him. God simply wants to use our past as a tool to shape us into His image.

How often do you live in the victories or defeats of yesterday? How often do you believe that your past defines who you are today? The memories of previous days can lull us into a deceptive complacency. God desires to shake our prideful perspective with the question, "Do you love Me more than your past?"

PAUL AND HIS PAST

Paul's life illustrates a noteworthy past of both good and evil deeds. He had accomplished much in the eyes of the religious, but he also wreaked havoc on the early church. In Philippians chapter three, Paul recounted his illustrious pedigree that impressed the religious elite. In these verses he enumerated his privileges.

> Philippians 3:4-8: *Though I might also have confidence in the flesh. If any other man thinketh that he hath whereof he might trust in the flesh, I more: Circumcised the eighth day, of the stock of Israel, of the tribe of Benjamin, an Hebrew of the Hebrews; as touching the law, a Pharisee; Concerning zeal, persecuting the church; touching the righteousness which is in the law, blameless. But what things were gain to me, those I counted loss for Christ. Yea doubtless, and I count all things but loss for the excellency of the knowledge of Christ Jesus my Lord: for whom I have suffered the loss of all things, and do count them but dung, that I may win Christ.*

Paul was circumcised the eighth day.

This ceremony began his elite upbringing and indicates that Paul was of Jewish-birth—not that he became a Jewish proselyte.

Paul was of the stock of Israel.

Paul had a noteworthy heritage of pure Jewish blood. His status was highly regarded and legally recognized.

Paul was of the tribe of Benjamin.

He could trace His prominent family to one of the sons of Rachel, not one of the maid-servants given to Jacob. The first king of Israel was in Paul's lineage. His tribe swore their allegiance to the house of David and ultimately to the Messiah.

Paul was a Hebrew of the Hebrews.

He held a highly respected Jewish status. Both of his parents were Jews. They retained their fathers' Hebrew language. They also remained Jewish in national heritage, religious beliefs, and ceremonial practices even when living in Tarsus.

Paul was a Pharisee in matters concerning the law.

His religious position was of the strictest sect. He zealously observed the law. He learned the law from the great Raban Gamaliel. In time, he could have become the high priest.

Paul displayed his zeal through persecuting the church.

Although Paul's past received great respect from the religious leaders of the day, he looked back on these privileges with regret. In his zeal, he had tried to eradicate the truth he had come to embrace. In spite of the great diligence and strictness he displayed, Paul's religious works were full of self-righteousness. He had considered himself blameless even when he gave his approval for the stoning of Stephen and the deaths of many others in the early church. The memory of the lives he had destroyed must have haunted him. The recollection of the arrests and imprisonment of the believers could have silenced him, if he had not turned his focus to the Savior and chosen to love Him more than the horrific memories.

When Paul met the Lord Jesus on the road to Damascus, his passion for the Savior immediately replaced his fervor for the Jewish law. Acts chapter nine gives us the story of Paul's encounter with God. On his way to persecute the church in Damascus, a bright light stopped Paul. The voice from heaven was unmistakably the voice of God and Paul's surrender was immediate and absolute. He became the messenger of the God he had tried so hard to silence.

He immediately preached Christ Jesus in the synagogues to the amazement of all. Through his missionary journeys and church planting endeavors, he reached multitudes with the gospel. Centuries later we learn of the Master through the pages of our Bible that Paul penned under the inspiration of the Holy Spirit.

Paul proved that his love for God was greater than either his positive or negative past. He did not let the honors of man or the sins of his flesh take precedent over his love for the Lord. His love for the Savior far exceeded his pride or his shame.

PAUL'S CREDENTIALS

Paul had the credentials to be confident in himself. His past led him down a religious road of great sacrifice and notoriety, but it was a path away from God. When he believed and received the Lord Jesus, he began a life of unmatched service. The accounts of his life of ministry and of his doctrinal instruction guide our lives through the inspired record of God's Word.

What about you? What would your list of accomplishments from the past look like? What do you consider as *gain* in your life? If we take Paul's full account into consideration, we realize that his reminiscing does not end with the praises of his accomplishments and our list should not end there either.

Philippians 3:7-8: *But what things were gain to me, those I counted loss for Christ. Yea doubtless, and I count all things but loss for the excellency of the knowledge of Christ Jesus my Lord: for whom I have suffered the loss of all things, and do count them but dung, that I may win Christ.*

When he contrasted his works with the knowledge and blessings of God, Paul counted all his accomplishments as worthless. No matter how impressive our religious résumé may appear, our labors are empty compared to knowing Christ and His work on our behalf. When we seek to know Him, we learn of His power through His resurrection and we experience an incredible fellowship through His suffering. Through that relationship with Christ, we find joy in serving Him. When we love Him supremely, our service becomes an offering of love to lay at His feet.

Do you know people who live in the past? They speak of their yesterdays as if they ended just moments ago. You probably have heard their stories before since their day-to-day reality is a captive of their memories. For some it is tales of amazing accomplishments that fill their thoughts with pride and self-worth. When insecurity threatens them, they resort to sharing the details of some marvelous memory once again. For others it is painful reminiscence of issues or events that have left scars that time cannot erase. The defeat is unending in their mind, and they seem unable to take that step beyond the pain, a step that would bring them healing and freedom to move on.

Whether the past is full of delightful memories or painful struggles, the past is still beyond the reach of today. In Philippians 3:13-14, Paul refers to the past with clear directions. He states that we are to "forget those things which are behind and reach forth unto those things which are before." The past cannot be undone or rewritten. Paul goes on to say that we should "press toward the mark for the prize of the high calling of God in Christ Jesus." With the past abandoned, we are more able to live today to God's glory.

MORE THAN MY PRESENT

During our years in South Carolina our family went through many transitions. When we moved there, our daughters were in high school and our son was upper elementary. As we moved to Wisconsin our family looked very different. Both of our daughters had graduated from high school and college and were married. They each had a beautiful little daughter. Our sons-in-laws were established in their occupations. Our son had graduated from high school and was almost finished with college. Many celebrations had taken place throughout these years. Many precious memories!

We were settling into the new life that these years had given to us. Our oldest daughter lived just a couple miles from us. She would bring Ella by to play with me while she went to the store. We would get together for Sunday dinner and little outings. What fun times we had!

Our daughter in Tennessee was only three hours away. Too far to just pop in, but close enough to easily plan visits. The day Karis was born we were holding her in our arms just hours after her birth. What a joy it was to be a grandmother—a grandmother close to her grandchildren.

I enjoyed my job at the Science Center. My schedule allowed for the flexibility I needed to continue writing and speaking. My ladies' Bible studies were going well; many young wives were beginning their families, and our Bible study ministered to their needs. It was the highlight of my week, and hopefully theirs too, as I shared God's Word with them.

But in spite of the joy of my present life, I knew God had called my husband to preach and one day we would go back into full-time ministry. When the day came for us to consider the move to Wisconsin, I realized I had to let go of the familiar world that had become so comfortable. My present life and ministry was changing drastically. To be obedient to the Lord, I had to be willing to leave my present life with granddaughters, co-workers, and Bible-study students and move to the unknown. What I was doing was sincere service to the Master; but open hands needed to be holding my service to Him. He determines the call; I must obey.

I probably could have defended the legitimacy of my service to God. I could have questioned God's plan to move us at such a time, but I would have planted seeds of doubt and confusion into the direct leading of God. I would have loved my current ministry and circumstances—no matter how virtuous I had made them sound—more than I loved my God.

Our current life and ministries can often make us content with where we are spiritually. This contentment slips into complacency and threatens our obedience to God's will. We may miss God's leading us to what He would have for us. We assume that our effectiveness has reached its full potential. When in reality, we have become complacent.

Another preacher, Philip, in the book of Acts sets an example for us of loving God more than the present. In Acts 8, Philip was preaching in the city of Samaria. People were responding to the heartfelt message Philip preached. Philip saw people healed of diseases and unclean spirits. These marvelous acts brought great rejoicing.

In the middle of revival, God sent an angel to give Philip his next assignment. He was to leave the excitement of this city and go to Gaza, a desert, and share the message of salvation with one man.

Leave the multitude for only one? Yes, Philip was to leave a productive ministry to go and speak with one man in his chariot. Philip obeyed God's call. He knew God's way was best.

When Philip met the man of Ethiopia, the man was reading from the book of Isaiah. The Ethiopian had no understanding of Isaiah's message. Philip joined him in the chariot, "opened his mouth, and began at the same scripture, and preached unto him Jesus" (Acts 8:35).

What a special mission God had for Philip. The power of the gospel reaches individuals as well as the masses. Through Philip's obedience, this man trusted Christ as Savior. If Philip had refused to leave the thriving ministry in Samaria, this man from Ethiopia would not have received the needed message.

Philip's love for God superseded his love for his present ministry to the multitude. Philip was willing and ready to follow God's call. His ministry was God's choosing. He would do what God called him to do because he loved God.

Philip's obedience challenges us to consider if we are satisfied and content with the status quo but missing the opportunities with a new, hungry believer. Do we love God more than our current ministry? Do we ignore His leading and remain where we are although He's clearly calling us to a new area of service?

May we forget the past's positives and negatives that we carry through our lives. May we focus on today, keeping our eyes on the Master and being willing to obey His leading even if it means making great changes.

I'm grateful that God gave me the grace to accept the changes in ministry that this move required. I thought I was sacrificing much to obey His call when instead He gave me many rich blessings.

In Wisconsin, I continue to teach Bible studies twice a month and a Sunday school class every week. I continue to travel and speak to new ladies in the churches and camps of the Midwest, and have had opportunities to speak internationally. I have the joy of loving a whole church full of ladies and their families. And I'm continuing to write.

Yes, I miss my family being close. I miss the dear ladies that I taught God's Word to. I miss the children that came to me on field trips. But God didn't take them away. He exchanged them for even more dear ones to show God's love. I don't know about you, but I don't want to miss God's assignments. May we show we love the Lord more than yesterday's memories or today's blessings by obediently following Him.

GOD'S LOVE IS ETERNAL

Jeremiah 31:3: The Lord hath appeared of old unto me, saying, Yea, I have loved thee with an everlasting love: therefore with lovingkindness have I drawn thee.

Although we can never fully comprehend His affection, we need to consider how God's love is expressed and declared in His Word. The love of this world is shallow and uncertain, but God's love is true and genuine. How magnificent His love! How feeble is ours!

God's love for us has no beginning and no ending. He loved us in eternity past; He loves us today; He will love us in the future. There has not been nor ever will there be a time that God does not love us.

When we strive to love Him as we should, we recognize how inferior our best efforts are. 1 John 4:19 states, "We love him, because he first loved us." God understands our inability to initiate and demonstrate such love. By His power, we are able to respond to His love first given to us. We should strive to love Him with a love that reflects His love to us.

CHAPTER 12
More Than my Future

ONE OF THE GREATEST UNCERTAINTIES of life is the future. No matter how unstable today may be, we at least can see and feel the details of the moment as we experience the events of the present. The future however is intangible. We can guess about the consequences that may face us in the near future; but we cannot know what tomorrow truly holds. Our best-laid plans are upended far too often. The unknown future can keep us overwhelmed and fearful.

How simple it all seemed as a little girl. "When I grow up, I'm going to be . . ." Remember those dreams? We were confident that we only needed to be older and taller. The occupations might vary from time to time, but the goal was the same—to do what we'd love to do and to be what we wanted to be. How simple it seemed. How many factors we couldn't comprehend.

Tomorrow.

What an impact it can have on today. It can steal our thoughts and energy and return us to reality feeling empty and hopeless. Whether we dream for tomorrow to come quicker or we fear what tomorrow may bring, our eyes are not fixed on the Savior when our focus is the future. We miss today's opportunity to love and serve the Master.

Do you have goals for tomorrow? Did that ambition begin at the feet of the Lord Jesus? Our plans may be exactly what God has for us, but is it the dream we long for or the Master? The future is our imagination. The Master, however, is ever by our side. Our love for Him should supersede all else and keep our attention on our Lord. Let's take a close look at what God says about loving things to come more than we love Him.

MORE THAN A FORWARD LOOK

In the fourth chapter of James, the author challenges us to look closely at the plans we create. How much regard are we giving to tomorrow? James states that many people plan without considering God's desires for them. Many worry about what might never occur. These believers were to be waiting on the Lord and not presuming upon or worrying over tomorrow. James directly addressed their boastful thoughts.

James 4:13-17: *Go to now, ye that say, To day or to morrow we will go into such a city, and continue there a year, and buy and sell, and get gain: Whereas ye know not what shall be on the morrow. For what is your life? It is even a vapour, that appeareth for a little time, and then vanisheth away. For that ye ought to say, If the Lord will, we shall live, and do this, or that. But now ye rejoice in your boastings: all such rejoicing is evil. Therefore to him that knoweth to do good, and doeth it not, to him it is sin.*

These merchants saw no need to depend on God. In fact, they believed their skills and plans were all that was necessary for success. Some of James's readers were saying that they planned to go into a particular city and stay for a year buying and selling and making great profit. Their plans did not include God, however, and they assumed that they had the power to make things happen exactly as they desired.

James brings the reader to the reality that no one knows what tomorrow will bring. Our life may end before tomorrow even begins. The events are beyond our control; we have no power over minutes, hours, days or years. Only God knows what the future holds; no one can boast of tomorrow.

The Bible gives other comparisons that express the fleeting moments of our lives.

Job 7:7a—*O remember that my life is wind...*

Psalm 102:3—*For my days are consumed like smoke and my bones are burned as an hearth*

1 Peter 1:24-25a—For all flesh is as grass and all the glory of man as the flower of grass. The grass withereth, and the flower thereof falleth away: But the Word of the Lord endureth for ever.

James 4:14b—For what is your life? It is even a vapour, that appeareth for a little time, and then vanisheth away.

God knows our future. Our days are under His loving guidance. No matter how uncertain our lives may be, we can rest confidently that He is in control. He asks us to humbly surrender our days to Him and not to boast of our elaborate plans. God wants us to be good stewards of each day and to love Him by surrendering to His plan for our tomorrows.

MORE THAN CLOSED DOORS—ACTS 16:1-11

When we sincerely seek God's will for the future, we may be overwhelmed when God shuts a door that we thought for sure He had opened.

This confusing disappointment faced Timothy, Paul, and Silas when they made their plans to go to Asia. In Acts 16:1-11, we learn that God closed the door for these men of God to go to Asia (verse 6) and Bithynia (verse 7). God did, however, lead the men to the place that He had chosen. Through a vision, Paul saw a man of Macedonia calling him to come and help. Paul and his team confidently obeyed and went to Macedonia knowing that God had called them to this needy area. To emphasize the importance of the mission and of their obedience, God shut two doors—Asia and Bithynia. The men had to keep their focus on obeying God and not on what seemed logical.

There were times during our years of waiting that I thought God was opening a door of ministry for us. Some of the places would have been big ministries with amazing opportunities. One particular ministry I knew well. The area was familiar and the people were my friends. It would be like going home, not only for me but also for my children.

The opportunity for me to serve again in this ministry would redeem a past of limited opportunity. I'd have much more to offer this time. How wonderful would it be to have a second chance, an occasion to redo part of my past. How often do you get a chance like that? I even found a clearly applicable Bible verse that pictured our return to this ministry. What a blessing it would be to anyone noting the comparison.

But God said, "No!"

Why had I wanted this familiar location to be our next ministry? After some prayer and thought, I realized it would have been easy. Yes, easy. Since when does God show Himself strong in the effortless things of my life? He shows His power in the difficult. Through my loss He gives the greatest gain. Why would I even want it to be simple? *Easy* would make me think I could do it on my own without His help.

I'm so grateful that God doesn't choose what I think is best. In the wearisome, the complicated, the demanding, He has the greatest opportunity to show Himself strong. Oh, that I would welcome the challenging! He promised His grace would be sufficient. The more sacrificial our task the greater display of His grace and glory.

The difference was evident when God opened the door to Wisconsin. The loving welcome we received gave us great confidence that God had opened this door. With the unfolding of the ministry throughout the following years, we understood the loving selection our Lord had made for us. I'm so glad my husband let God choose for us . . . and not me.

If we love our future plans more than we love God, we will be devastated if God shuts the door to those plans. The disappointment can shake the foundation of our faith and our desire to serve. Loving God means we will hold onto our future plans loosely. If God shuts the door or leads us on, we must obey and accept His will with a gracious spirit.

We should be ready and willing to follow Him wherever and whenever He leads. He wants our obedience, trust, and supreme love. We should accept the closed doors with the same graciousness that we accept the doors of fruitful ministry that He sends us through.

MORE THAN SELFISH PLANS

Loving God more than our future also includes loving God more than our self-centered plans. How often do we make and implement our ideas without consulting our Lord? We become too headstrong, foolish, and proud to change our course. Would someone really love their desires for their future more than they love the Lord Jesus?

Jesus gave us an account of a man who made his future his priority. He was a rich man, a landowner, who had an exceptional harvest. His efforts had yielded a crop that exceeded his planning and preparation. Instead of being a wise steward and sharing his abundance with others who were in need, he determined to keep all the harvest for himself. To safely store the bumper crop, he ordered his old barns torn down and newer, bigger ones built. He looked forward to days to eat, drink and be merry. By the time the harvest was complete so were the barns.

This foolish man's plans excluded God. His love for the material gain outweighed his love for God. His wealth could not save his soul nor spare his life. His efforts to preserve his future were futile. God ended the farmer's life that night.

This man's love for himself and earthly riches, as well as his future, were far greater than his love for God. He could not see the needs of the moment, only his plan for the future. When we love our plans for the future more than we love God, we, too, are foolish in God's economy.

The future lies just beyond our grasp. We may try to catch a glimpse of it from today, but only God knows what will be beyond this moment.

One time this truth left me very unsettled. Our nation had reelected a president whose agenda was far from the biblical principles that are the foundation of our government. With no regard for the true needs of our land, the President and Congress began to rapidly implement the extreme agenda that they had only tiptoed around in the President's first term.

I found myself afraid. What was our nation to become? Where were we headed? The predictions were devastating. My heart began to fear for my children and grandchildren. Socialistic tenants have begun to replace scripturally founded practices. What will these changes do to our futures? A sense of panic overcame my heart.

The Lord rebuked my fearful thinking. His reassurance was amazing as He led me to remember that He was in control.

God holds the future. I simply must keep my focus on Him and obediently follow His leading. Even with trying days, His Word can flourish in my heart.

Our mandate, our calling from God, is unchanged. We are to love the Lord our God with all our heart, all our soul, all our mind, and all our strength (Mark 12:30). Secondly, we are to love our neighbor as ourselves. There is no need to worry about tomorrow. God is in control. He will give the necessary grace to endure whatever lies ahead. We must focus on the Lord Jesus and keep our eyes fixed on Him. With this love and focus in place, we will not allow the worry of tomorrow to surpass our love for the Master today.

GOD'S LOVE EVIDENCED

Ephesians 3:20: *Now unto him that is able to do exceeding abundantly above all that we ask or think, according to the power that worketh in us.*

Far too often our lack of faith hinders God's working in our lives. We miss the abundance of His blessings because we place unwarranted limits on God's ability to work and bless. The precious words of Ephesians 3:20 clarify what God wants to do in each of our lives.

Take a look at the meaning of some key words in Ephesians 3:20.

Able means to be capable, strong, and powerful.

Exceeding means over, beyond, and more than.

Abundantly means over and above, much more than all.

Above means more or beyond, over.

All means everything.

This verse declares that God is able to do what "we ask or think." That phrase alone should give us confidence and rest in the love of God. But the verse says so much more. It says "all that we ask or think" He is capable of doing. But still that's not the whole meaning. The verse takes it much further with the preceding words. God is "able to do **exceeding abundantly above all** that we ask or think." Because of His great love for us, He wants to work in ways that greatly exceed the need that we think we have. How amazing is His matchless love that is evidenced in His abundant blessing! Let us rest in His gracious provision and care for all our tomorrows.

CHAPTER 13

What Now?

MY LIFE HAS BEEN LIVED mostly in small towns. Some towns were larger than others, but all shared the quaint small-town feeling. My experience with a farm is very limited. Even now as we travel the roads of Wisconsin, I'm fascinated with the red barns, pastures, and cattle that define the countryside.

My limited experience of farm life revolves around my grandparents' farm in southern Michigan. From my earliest memories, I recall Grandma busy about her kitchen. An electric stove never replaced her wood-burning cook stove. No matter what the temperature inside or out, the fire in Grandma's stove would be ablaze as she went about her kitchen duties. Grandma's kitchen was her domain and nothing interfered with the efficiency of her chores or meal preparations.

I was always astounded when Grandma let Grandpa bring the tiny lambs into the kitchen for my sisters and me to see. My quiet, yet strong, grandfather overruled Grandma's protests of lambs invading her tidy kitchen. We little citified granddaughters adored the spring lambs. What a thrill to closely see these woolly creatures. Pictures document us admiring the precious newborn lambs by the warmth of Grandma's antique stove.

Grandpa's heart reflected the heart of a shepherd. His gentle but firm hold on the nervous creatures calmed their fears as they surveyed their strange surroundings. No objection from Grandma prevented him from sharing these precious babies with us. These special moments with Grandpa's lambs come immediately to mind as I read this passage.

After each question, Jesus gave Peter a life-changing command "Feed my lambs . . . feed my sheep" (John 21:15-17).

The repetition of Jesus' words was significant. Jesus wanted this message to penetrate Peter's heart and ours as well. To daily apply and obey this directive, God calls us to seek the lost, sustain the lambs, and surrender the loved.

SEEK THE LOST

Jesus' command to feed the sheep included Peter seeking those who did not know the truth about Jesus. When Jesus invited Peter to follow Him, He was calling a fisherman to become a fisher of men. Peter was to share the message of the cross with those who did not know Jesus as the Messiah, the Savior.

> Matthew 4:18-20: *And Jesus, walking by the sea of Galilee, saw two brethren, Simon called Peter, and Andrew his brother, casting a net into the sea: for they were fishers. And he saith unto them, Follow me, and I will make you fishers of men. And they straightway left their nets, and followed him.*

In John 21, Jesus reiterated His call to Peter. Peter was to spend his life proclaiming the message of the cross. Whether to thousands of people gathered in Jerusalem for Pentecost (Act 2) or to a lame man begging at the gate of the temple (Acts 3), his calling was clear. Peter was to teach and preach the Lord Jesus. He was to focus on spreading the good news of salvation throughout the land.

Jesus told a parable in Luke 15:3-7 about a shepherd and his sheep. Only one sheep of the entire flock was missing, yet the shepherd could not be satisfied until all were safely home. He left the ninety-nine sheep in the fold to go find the one. The loving Shepherd found the wayward lamb and safely carried it back to the others.

What was lost was found! Jesus wanted Peter to have the compassion of the Shepherd and be ready to minister to those around him who had never heard the truths of salvation. Peter's call to "feed the lambs" is our calling too. The great commission given at the end of the Gospels is as much to us as it was to the apostles.

Matthew 28:19-20: *Go ye therefore, and teach all nations, baptizing them in the name of the Father, and of the Son, and of the Holy Ghost: Teaching them to observe all things whatsoever I have commanded you: and, lo, I am with you alway, even unto the end of the world. Amen.*

Many times we overlook the opportunities God gives us to share His truth with those around us. We become so distracted with the cares of our daily routine that we miss these precious occasions to witness or disciple. What seems like an interruption can actually be a treasured moment for God's glory.

The house we purchased in Wisconsin was built in 1901. The remodeled rooms cannot hide the years of heritage that match our quaint little town. One unique feature is the driveway we share with our neighbor. In the early years of the twentieth century, there was no need for driveways and garages, so when the need arose the solution was a shared driveway to allow both houses to have a place to park off the street and for access to garages built behind the houses. The establishing of our home in Wisconsin included building a friendship with the couple with whom we shared the driveway.

My neighbor had completed a course of study that had added months of class hours to her full-time job. I had a congratulations card and plate of cookies waiting to help her celebrate. I'd been watching for her to arrive home so I could run my gift over to her.

When I walked into the kitchen late one afternoon, she was heading for her car. I quickly donned my coat and ran out to give her my little present. She gratefully received my home-baked goodies and well wishes. She then proceeded to ask me a question that only the gospel could answer.

An hour later she left my kitchen with the gospel message as clearly presented as I knew how. She left without trusting Christ as Savior, but with a time appointed on Thursday to meet again. Was this my plan for this Tuesday afternoon? Not really. But I walked through the door that He opened.

No chore completed compares to sharing the message of the cross. What a precious interruption. What a joy it was to see her receive Christ as Savior a short time later. We spent many more hours at my kitchen table studying God's Word. She was a precious lamb that I had the joy of feeding.

May the Lord forgive us for the times that we are so focused on our chosen activities that we miss the opportunities He gives us to minister to those around us. May we always be willing to set aside our plans for His.

SUSTAIN THE LAMBS

God expects His children to grow in grace and in the knowledge of His Word. No matter how long we live, we should be constantly growing in our Christlikeness. We should be growing in our understanding and knowledge of God. He has given us His precious Word that we might better know Him and trust Him. God has also given us pastors to teach us the truths of God's Word and challenge our hearts to greater surrender and obedience. Through the faithful preaching and teaching of God's Word, we grow in our understanding of God and His truth. Isaiah gave a beautiful picture of what God expects from His leaders.

Isaiah 40:11: *He shall feed his flock like a shepherd: he shall gather the lambs with his arm, and carry them in his bosom, and shall gently lead those that are with young.*

What about us? What is a woman's role in God's plan for sustaining the lambs? Titus 2:3-5 directs the older women to teach and minister to younger women. While under the authority and teaching of godly husbands and pastors, God commands women to pass along the practical truths of God's Word to those that are younger.

Titus 2:3-5: *The aged women likewise, that they be in behaviour as becometh holiness, not false accusers, not given to much wine, teachers of good things.*

This instruction is not necessarily in a formal teaching setting, although there are times and places for this kind of training. Probably the greatest platform for this exchange is the younger women observing the older women. No matter how old we are, there is someone younger watching us. Whatever our role within the community, church family, neighborhood, or workplace, some younger woman or girl is watching our reactions and actions as an older woman. She is noting our choice of words, attitudes, and demeanor.

What are we feeding the lambs around us? Are we exemplifying godliness? Throughout the years, I've seen many who are unaware of the impact that they are making.

We don't have to wonder what God would have us feed these precious lambs. Titus 2 clearly gives the character we are to display and the curriculum we are to teach to the younger women.

Titus 2:4-5: *That they may teach the young women to be sober, to love their husbands, to love their children, To be discreet, chaste, keepers at home, good, obedient to their own husbands, that the word of God be not blasphemed.*

There is much to learn! No one is exempt from both learning and teaching. No matter how long ago we trusted Christ as Savior, we need to strive to be closer to the Savior today than we were yesterday. We need to diligently study His Word and endeavor to take the truths we learn and turn them into daily actions that demonstrate the goodness of our God. God has made our responsibility clear.

The lambs that need to be fed are all those who have trusted the Lord in recent months or those who have never grown beyond their salvation. Both need the simplicity of the Word of God given to them. Peter describes this truth as milk. In 1 Peter 2:2, He states that, "As newborn babes, desire the sincere milk of the word, that ye may grow thereby."

Have you seen a hungry little baby lately? I have seen that intense desire for food in my children and now in my grandchildren. You know the look. Their little mouths are frantically searching for nourishment. This inevitable search is only satisfied when they receive what they long for.

The same is true for Christians. Many are searching to know God and new believers of any age need the "milk" of the Word, the simple promises and truths of Scripture. As a baby enjoys that precious milk, the new believer rests in the scores of foundational truths that she can comprehend.

Our responsibility to teach the younger women is not limited to new believers. When Jesus told Peter to feed the sheep in John 21:16, He was commanding Peter to also feed the mature believers who needed to go deeper into God's Word. The strong meat of the Word needs to be given "to them that are of full age, even those who by reason of use have their senses exercised to discern both good and evil" (Hebrews 5:14). Proverbs 27:17 tells us to "sharpen the countenance" of our friends. This accountability to each other is the responsibility of all mature believers. We are to be challenging our friends to a greater devotion to God, a greater knowledge of Him, and a greater application of the Word to our daily lives.

Jesus commanded Peter to keep his focus on the service that God had called him, the nurturing of the lambs and sheep—both new and mature believers. Through the chapters of First and Second Peter, Peter challenges us to be ready for the suffering and trials that this life brings.

Our salvation is firmly resting in the finished work of Jesus on the cross and His resurrection from the dead. We have a great hope to give to others. May we challenge those around us to "grow in grace and in the knowledge of our Lord and Savior Jesus Christ" (2 Peter 3:18).

There is no greater joy than sharing the good news of salvation and having that person accept Jesus Christ as their personal Savior. The Shepherd rejoiced when the lost lamb was found, and he led his neighbors and friends to rejoice with him. May we show a heart of gratitude and a spirit of praise for what the Lord has done when a person accepts Christ as their Savior.

SURRENDER THE LOVED

The greatest test of our love to the Lord is in releasing to His care those we love dearly, but seem helpless to minister to. Our ability to "feed" them is ineffective. We have nothing more to give or share.

We can feed these sheep by giving them to the Lord and allowing Him to work in their hearts. It is then our ministry becomes one of intercession. We take them before the Lord in ceaseless prayer.

In Genesis 22:1-19, we have an amazing story of a father's obedience and love. The account pictures the surrender of the loved. God asked Abraham to offer his only son, Isaac, on an altar instead of sacrificing a lamb. After twenty-five years of waiting for God to send the promised heir, Isaac was finally born when Abraham was one hundred years old and Sarah was ninety. Now, with Isaac no more than twenty years old, God told Abraham to take Isaac to Mount Moriah and offer him as a sacrifice instead of the usual lamb.

Abraham obeyed God. He took Isaac and three servants and began the long journey to the mountain God had selected. Abraham laid the wood in order, bound the hands of Isaac the promised heir, and placed him on the altar. Abraham loved God more than he loved Isaac, but Abraham also knew that God loved Isaac more than he did. He could trust God with Isaac's life.

When the knife was about to take the life of Abraham's precious son, God stopped Abraham. God declared that now He knew Abraham loved Him more than he loved Isaac. Abraham was willing to give to God what was most precious to him—his son, Isaac.

I have realized that there are times in our lives that God asks us to lay our *Isaac* upon the altar. Of course this is not the literal sacrifice that He asked Abraham to offer, but the sacrifice is just a significant. Your Isaac looks different than mine, but maybe there is someone that you must lay before the Lord for Him to take care of because you no longer can. It is now up to God to directly work in their life. You can only step back and watch God bring the deliverance.

To answer this question, "Lovest thou me more than these?" from the depths of our heart may involve the sacrificial releasing of this *lamb* that we love so deeply to God.

Who is it in your life that you must release to God's care? Feeding the sheep at times includes stepping back and letting God work. I challenge you. Lay your Isaac down and let God bring the victory in their lives in His time and in His way.

LOVE AS HE LOVED

John 13:34: *A new commandment I give unto you, That ye love one another; as I have loved you, that ye also love one another.*

The following statements summarize how God's love toward us will affect how we love those around us. Read through each statement slowly and decide if you love others as the Lord Jesus would have you to. This kind of love only happens when we surrender to God and let Him love others through us.

If I love others as God loves me, I will love them no matter what they do. That's how God loves me.

If I love others as God loves me, I will not feel threatened by them. I will love them without fearing their actions or words.

If I love others as God loves me, I will love them where they are and allow God to stretch my love.

If I love others as God loves me, I will patiently endure whatever pain or irritation they may bring me.

When we realize the enormity of the love of God for us, we also get a glimpse of what He desires to do on our behalf. This level of love gives to the one loved whatever the cost may be. When we became His child at salvation, we received His love and grace. Through time in the Word, we get to know our precious Savior better and understand His desire to work in marvelous ways in our life. His great love is demonstrated in His daily provision, gracious care, and unconditional love. When we begin to comprehend His love for us, our hearts should desire to share His love with others.

CHAPTER 14

Thou Knowest that I Love Thee

THE YEARS HAVE QUICKLY PASSED since our arrival to Wisconsin. What sweet years they have been. Our church people have become not just our congregation to minister to, but also our family in the Lord to love. Our quaint little town has become our home.

God's loving hand has grown us to a greater understanding of His love and goodness. The blessings have been abundant. Our lives continue to change by the Holy Spirit using God's Word to mold and shape us. We have witnessed trials that have left an impact. The impact demands an even greater love for God and greater understanding of His precious truths.

One thing remains unchanged. God continues to ask me if I love Him most. The need to evaluate the priority of my love is never far from my reality. Loving God more than anything or anyone requires a constant focus. When I settle into the routine of life, challenges occur. I once again must face the choice of accepting God's will and keeping my love for Him supreme or of letting something else steal my heart.

The choices that this life of obedience requires are constant. To a bystander it may look simple, but obedience to God is challenging. Everything around me promotes following my heart, doing what feels best, or having it my way. None of these approaches to life lead me to a path of obedience to God. Only through determined, purposeful decisions can I walk a path that reflects a supreme love for God. God gives me victory in certain areas of my life by a onetime surrender. Other areas I must constantly revisit and put them in their proper place.

Perhaps there are areas of your life beyond what we have considered that require evaluation. We have contemplated enough examples to illustrate this crucial perspective. Does the question, "Lovest thou me more than these?" reveal the dilemma of your heart?

MY LOVE FOR MY FAMILY

Of all the areas of surrender that I have considered, my greatest struggle is my love for my family. My love for them is constantly seeking to take the place in my life that only God deserves. God's grace is faithful each time my heart longs for the miles to be fewer between us. When we are together and the moment to say good-bye arrives, God floods me with His grace. Oh, the tears still flow, but God carries me through with a gentle, gracious peace that reassures me of His love and understanding. He gives me the courage to face the separation once again.

Some significant events in our children's lives have given me reassurance that our obedience to God was the right example. I realize that our decisions did not directly link to their obedience; but if I had refused to love God *more than these* would my example of disobedience have hindered their obedience?

A couple years after we moved to Wisconsin, our son-in-law and daughter began hosting a Bible study in their home. The young families that attended soon filled and overflowed the space. The Lord allowed them to purchase a larger home that sufficiently accommodated the families attending. My daughter and son-in-law were grateful for the extra space for their family, but their ministry to these young families was a factor they considered when they decided on a new home. Not only does this home comfortably allow for parents to study God's Word, their children can easily have their own Bible time as well.

Our daughter and her family that were in Tennessee ministering in a church felt the Lord calling them to church planting. They along with two other families obeyed God's call to start a church in the center of a large western city. They packed up their possessions, shared their new ministry in some churches, and went out West. Their church today has nearly three hundred people attending and a great building in a marvelous location.

God blessed both of these homes and our whole family with the miraculous births and adoptions of five more little grandchildren since we moved to Wisconsin. Although we were not able to be there within hours of all of their arrivals, it wasn't long before we held each one and welcomed them into our family. God has blessed us with many precious moments.

During these years, our son went through a season of spiritual struggle as he completed college and entered the work force. The distance was especially painful as we recognized the dark place where he was. Daily for several years, my heart agonized in prayer for our son. My heart struggled to not let this precious son become an idol. It was easy to let my concern for him consume my every thought. God convicted me many times about how I was spending more time thinking about my son than I was thinking of Him. I had to consciously make a choice to love God more than my son. I had to deliberately place him in God's hands.

Throughout the entire time of his struggle, he never lost contact with his family. God allowed us the joy of continuing to share God's love and ours with him and graciously answered our prayers. God used a variety of circumstances to bring our son back to Himself.

As the godly men in his church surrounded our son in biblical love, he began to grow in grace. He became very successful in the business world and quickly began to advance in his company. The higher he went, though, the more unsettled he became. God was calling him to Asia. Jon left his job and all the success he had obtained, and went to Hong Kong to teach English to children. He not only shares the beauty of our language, but also the message of the Savior with his little students.

Jon recently married a beautiful Christian lady from Hong Kong. She is a precious addition to our family. God has given them a heart for the world. We are excited to see how God is using them as He unfolds His precious plans for them.

When I look at what God has done in our family these past years, I cannot help but wonder how different it might have been if I had not been willing to love God enough to move to Wisconsin. God has asked our children to make significant changes. Would they have been as quick to obey if I had resisted God's leading in my life?

I am so grateful that they each have chosen to obey God. Ultimately they are answerable to God for their choices, but I pray that my efforts to follow the Savior encouraged them to obey His leading in their lives.

MY LOVE FOR MY CO-WORKERS

Thanks to social networking opportunities, I have been able to stay in touch with many of my southern friends both from work and church. I enjoy seeing the pictures of them with their families and am often amazed to see how their children have grown. The passage of time is best indicated by the changes in children.

Not all the news is fun and exciting. Several of my co-workers from the science center shared the sad news that my supervisor was diagnosed with a terminal disease. She and I had worked closely throughout my years teaching there. I sent her a card and a personal note expressing my love and prayers for her. The message of her illness and then of her death arrived so close together that it seemed surreal. My heart grieved when I heard the news. I was glad I had written to her and hoped that my card had arrived in time for my message to encourage her heart. This friend had come to church with me several times. I knew she had heard the gospel preached on those Sundays, and I prayed she had seen me live it out before her. I have to ask myself though, did I do all I could to help her understand the gift of salvation?

I have heard from other friends throughout these years with questions about the burdens they were facing or with prayer requests to add to my time with the Lord. I've received phone calls of discouragement and others of joy. For these incidents, I have tried to transmit all the love and encouragement that is possible to send through the phone. Nothing like a literal hug, but hopefully close.

MY LOVE FOR MY MINISTRIES

I am amazed how God continues to expand my sphere of influence. He has opened doors of opportunity for me to share Him and His Word. All the ministries that I thought I was sacrificing with moving north have been given back to me in abundance. Each year my speaking schedule has increased. My opportunities have even extended to international settings. I have had the privilege to share God's precious Word through the voice of a translator.

MY RELIEF FROM FEAR

God takes my fears and shows His power and strength. Whether my fears are from without or within, He faithfully sustains me and proves His love and goodness. The personal trials continue to come into my life; but He daily brings me to His side in sweet victory when I yield to His working and surrender to His desires.

I could go through the topic of each chapter and recount the lessons that led to blessings. God is faithful. When we strive to keep Him first, He takes our feeble efforts and multiplies them for His glory. When we fail, He is ready to forgive and to continue His work in our lives.

"Do you love Me more than these?" This question asked that morning on the seashore has become a part of my life. No matter where God leads my family or me in the days ahead, I can be confident that His love and presence will never leave me. I am amazed that this question continues to be such a crucial factor in my life.

I don't know what God has planned for the days ahead, but I know that in the midst of the decisions this priority must be secure. Although my husband and I will soon face the age of accepted retirement, we see God using us and leading us in ways that many young people would be hesitant to undertake.

Over the last couple years, God has increased my vision for the world. With the opportunities to travel and minister internationally, my heart has grown along with the expanding vision. I'm not sure how God will use me in the days ahead, but I see Him leading and directing my heart to women far beyond my Midwest home. And I am once again faced with the daunting question of my love for God. Will I love Him most and obey His call?

To walk in obedience on the path the Lord has prepared means I must trust Him and keep my focus and love directed. He will receive glory because I choose to walk the path of loving Him above all else. God's grace will always match my need. How can I help but love Him above all else?

I don't know how many years of life lie ahead of me, but one thing I know: I want to serve and love my Lord above all else right to the end. Until the day He calls me home, may I be faithful to love Him above all else. May my life bring Him great glory!

I hope you have learned much from the study of this passage. The truths I've shared are not just for the momentous times of our lives. The everyday tasks need to be done with the same emphasis

How would you answer Jesus' question?

What are you tempted to love more than the Savior?

Only you can determine your "these" and by God's grace, His enabling power, love Him supremely. When our hearts are in conflict between God and this world, I pray that our choice will be to love God with a love truly greater than "all of these!"

John 21:17: *He saith unto him the third time, Simon, son of Jonas, lovest thou me? . . .. And he said unto him, Lord, thou knowest all things; thou knowest that I love thee. Jesus saith unto him, Feed my sheep.*

MORE THAN THESE
Study Questions

CHAPTER 1—MY LOVE TESTED

This book is more than just a personal accounting of what God did in my heart as we began a new ministry. The applications are endless when we consider our love for the Lord Jesus. It is important to regularly evaluate our walk with the Lord. Satan works tirelessly to make us doubt our relationship to the Savior and our obedience to His Word. Please consider the questions designed to follow each chapter. The application of these biblical truths to your own heart and situation is crucial if you are to genuinely consider your love for the Savior.

Please read John 21. Fill in the details of the various events of that day.

John 21:1-8—The disciples go fishing

John 21:9-14—Jesus provides for the fishermen

John 21:15-23—Jesus asks Peter three crucial questions.

What honestly would have been your answer to Jesus if He asked you this question instead of Peter? *Some times I think I do — but really it is all about me*

What do you hope to learn from this study? *How to really love Jesus with all my heart. To really put & Love Jesus above all else*

145

Memorize: Mark 12:30: "And thou shalt love the Lord thy God with all thy heart, and with all thy soul, and with all thy mind, and with all thy strength: this is the first commandment."

Prayer Time: Take a few minutes to pray asking the Lord to help you honestly face the needs of your heart as you read this book and answer these questions.

CHAPTER 2—LOVEST THOU ME?

The disciples became weary as they waited for Jesus. After three years at Jesus' side ministering to the multitudes, the last thing they wanted was to return to fishing. Yet, in this time of unknown waiting, they returned to the familiar. It was in this time of the mundane that the Lord Jesus directed them to their ultimate mission—to love Him above all and be only fishers of men.

Read John 21:1-8. What do these verses teach us about being weary in the midst of the wait? *Start doing what we know.*

Galatians 6:9 *Dont become weary of doing good in due time we will reap - Dont*

Isaiah 40:31 *lose heart. Wait on the Lord - Dont lose heart in due time wings like Eagles run + not be weary"*

What was Jesus wanting Peter to consider? *To total Commit to Him*

Did Jesus know the state of Peter's heart? *yes*

John 2:25 *He knows our hearts*

John 21:17 *Peter wanted to but he was weak as we are. Jesus gives us strength*

How should you respond to seasons of waiting? *Continue to wait - believe & Pray*

Does the Lord know the state of your heart? How would the Lord Jesus describe your heart? *weak, desire yes to know Christ + obey but uncertain*

Memorize: Mark 12:30: "And thou shalt love the Lord thy God with all thy heart, and with all thy soul, and with all thy mind, and with all thy strength: this is the first commandment."

Prayer Time: Take a few minutes to pray asking the Lord to help you honestly evaluate your love for Him.

CHAPTER 3—MORE THAN THESE

The first time that Jesus asked Peter this question, He included a comparison—"Lovest thou me more than these?" Jesus was asking Peter to compare his love for Him to his love for other things or people in his life. What is your "these?" Yours is probably different than mine. But all of us have good, God-given things or people in our lives that we are tempted to love with a love that only the Lord deserves.

Read John 21:9-13. What was Jesus' first concern for these men? *They had food to eat*

List the things or people in your life that you are tempted to love more than God. *my girls & their family - friends*

God wants you to honestly assess the state of your heart. What do these verses tell you about your heart?

Proverbs 4:23 *keep your heart with all diligence For out of it springs the issue of life*

Jeremiah 17:9 *The heart is deceitful above all things + desperately wicked Who can know it?*

Matthew 15:18-19 *But those things which proceed out of the mouth come from the heart, and they defile a man. Heart evil*

Why is it extremely important to honestly face the truth about your heart? *So we can ask Jesus for help to clean us up.*

How are you to walk before the Lord?

Habakkuk 2:4 *Behold the proud. His soul is not upright in him. But the just shall live by faith in*

2 Corinthians 5:7 *For we walk by faith + not by sight*

What people or things in your life could be considered an idol because it/they have taken a place in your heart that only God should have?

Memorize: Mark 12:30: "And thou shalt love the Lord thy God with all thy heart, and with all thy soul, and with all thy mind, and with all thy strength: this is the first commandment."

h s m s

Prayer Time: Take a few minutes to pray asking the Lord to help you honestly evaluate the needs of your heart and your walk with Him.

CHAPTER 4—MORE THAN FAMILY

Because our family is the most valuable gift that God gives us, our greatest temptation may be to let these dear ones usurp the throne of our heart. God wants us to love our family, but our love for family must not supersede our love for Him. We are to be faithful stewards of His precious gifts to us, but we are never to let those gifts become idols.

What does Jesus teach us in Luke 14:26 and Matthew 10:37 about our love for others compared to our love for Him?

Read 1 Samuel 1. How does Hannah picture a mother who loved God more than she loved her son?

Read 1 Samuel 2:1-10. Hannah's knowledge of God was great. List the names and descriptions of God that she used in her song of praise as she left little Samuel in the temple.

Read through the list of statements about your child being your idol. Are some of these true of you and your children?

Memorize: Mark 12:30: "And thou shalt love the Lord thy God with all thy heart, and with all thy soul, and with all thy mind, and with all thy strength: this is the first commandment."

Prayer Time: Take a few minutes to pray praising God for the family He has given you. Ask the Lord to help you put your family in their proper place in your heart.

CHAPTER 5—MORE THAN FRIENDS

Family may be the most obvious group of people that we are tempted to love more than we love God. Our friends and co-workers also may be stealing your love from the Savior. They may have more influence in your life than you realize. Your co-workers and friends may be silencing your witness.

Read Acts 10:24-27 and Acts 12:21-23. Compare Peter's and Herod's response to the praise of men. List the differences.

How can you practically apply the truths in Matthew 10:32-33 to your everyday life?

In Matthew 5:13-15, the believer is pictured as salt and light. How are you being salt and light to those around you? In what ways do you need to strive to better by God's grace?

Proverbs 18:24 tells us how we can make friends and then that God is closer than a brother. How are you growing that friendship with God? Through His Word? Through prayer? How are you befriending others for God's glory?

Memorize: Mark 12:30: "And thou shalt love the Lord thy God with all thy heart, and with all thy soul, and with all thy mind, and with all thy strength: this is the first commandment."

Prayer Time: Take a few minutes to pray praising God for the friends He has given you. Ask the Lord to help you be the salt and light to all that you are around.

CHAPTER 6—MORE THAN POSSESSIONS

Sometimes it's not other people that draw our heart and love from the Lord. You may be consciously building the right priorities into your relationships, but the things of this world have captured your heart. Even common things, seeming necessities, may have taken the place of the Lord Jesus in your priorities.

In Hebrews 13:5, what is the prerequisite for contentment?

Don't have covetousness - be content He will never leave us

1 Timothy 6:11, 17-19 gives a list of guidelines that we should follow to keep our possessions in the proper place. What do you learn about each of these guidelines in the verses indicated?

Righteousness—Romans 8:4 *walks after the Spirit*

Godliness—1 Timothy 6:6 *godliness with contentment is great gain*

Faith—2 Corinthians 5:7 *we walk by faith now by sight*

Love—John 13:34-35 *Love one another as Jesus has love us*

Patience—Colossians 1:11 *strength with all power unto all patience & long suffering with joyfulness*

Meekness—Titus 3:2 *Speak no evil of man - no brawler, gentle meekness to all.*

Humility—James 4:6 *Give more grace - resist the proud - give grace to the humble*

Generosity—2 Corinthians 9:7 *Give generous. God loves a cheerful giver*

Would you say you are more like the rich young ruler or the disciples?

(Luke 18:18-30) *afraid more like the young ruler.*

Memorize: Deuteronomy 10:12: "And now, Israel, what doth the Lord thy God require of thee, but to fear the Lord thy God, to walk in all his ways, and to love him, and to serve the Lord thy God with all thy heart and with all thy soul."

Prayer Time: Take a few minutes to pray praising God for all He has given you. Ask the Lord to help you be grateful, content, and generous with all He has given you.

CHAPTER 7—MORE THAN MYSELF

If we are to take up our cross, we are going to have to unreservedly surrender to God. Whatever our abilities, strengths, and weakness, we give them to Him. We must denying ourselves completely and completely surrender to Him. When a woman denies herself and takes up her cross, only then is she prepared to follow Jesus as He desires.

How is Philippians 2:7-8 pictured in John 13:1-5?

Read Romans 12:1-3. These verses explain our surrender that God desires. What words describe this surrender?

Our bodies were instruments of sin before we trusted the Lord Jesus as our Savior. God wants our bodies to be surrendered to Him to be a pathway through which He can be seen. How does Romans 12:2 describe the changes?

The world around us shapes our thinking, values, and even our actions. How does God stop that conforming process when we surrender to Him?

How does 1 Peter 1:13-15 describe this change?

How is God's will described in Romans 12:2?

Memorize: Deuteronomy 10:12: "And now, Israel, what doth the Lord thy God require of thee, but to fear the Lord thy God, to walk in all his ways, and to love him, and to serve the Lord thy God with all thy heart and with all thy soul."

Prayer Time: Ask God to show you the areas of your life that you still need to surrender to Him. Humbly ask His forgiveness for thinking of yourself more highly that you should. Welcome His working in your body, mind and heart.

CHAPTER 8—MORE THAN MY FEARS FROM WITHOUT

God's Word tells us how we can be free from fear. 2 Timothy 1:7 declares that God has not given us this spirit of fear. His gifts of power, love and a sound mind will only occupy a heart that gives those fears to Him. This freedom is not the absence of problems or trials but a peace in the midst of the trial. That peace comes from a relationship with God and confidence in God.

Review the three truths about God.

God is. I must strive to know Him better. (Philippians 3:10)

God can. I must trust Him without reservation. (Psalm 40:5)

God will. I must rest in His unfailing promises. (Jeremiah 33:3)

Exodus 15 gives the song Moses sang after he and the Hebrew nation crossed the Red Sea. Find examples of "God is, God can, and God will" in this passage.

EXODUS 15	V. 2
	V. 3
GOD IS	V. 6
	V. 7
	V. 11
	V. 13
	V. 21
GOD CAN	V. 7
	V. 14-16
GOD WILL	V. 8-10, 19
	V. 13
	V. 14-16

Memorize: Jeremiah 33:3: "Call unto me, and I will answer thee, and show thee great and mighty things, which thou knowest not."

Prayer Time: Praise God for who He is, for what He can do, and for what He will do! Praise Him for being greater than any fear!

CHAPTER 9—MORE THAN MY FEAR OF CIRCUMSTANCES

There are many circumstances in life that are beyond our control. In spite of our detailed organizing and planning, life brings us many unexpected, unstoppable, unalterable events. The actions and decisions of others can change the course of our lives at a moment's notice. Our helplessness can be overwhelming. It is at these moments that our confidence in God is put to the test.

In the following verses, what is gained through trials and suffering?

2 Corinthians 1:3-5

2 Timothy 3:10-11

James 1:3-5

James 1:12

1 Peter 1:7

1 Peter 2:19-20

1 Peter 4:12-14

Memorize: Jeremiah 33:3: "Call unto me, and I will answer thee, and show thee great and mighty things, which thou knowest not."

Prayer Time: Praise God for His control and power over all things. Confess your fears to Him. Praise Him for being greater than any fear.

CHAPTER 10—MORE THAN MY FEAR OF THE UNKNOWN

The older we grow and the more people in our lives, the greater our fear of the unknown can become. Those of us with children and grandchildren look at this world and fear can easily overtake us. What will life be like for our little ones by the time they are adults? Fearful unknowns can replace our creative imaginations.

In the following passages, well-known Bible characters faced serious issues. The outcome of their circumstances was unknown when they had to make a decision about their actions. Read the passages, note the person(s) involved and the situation with an unknown factor.

Passage	Person(s)	Unknown Factor
Exodus 2:1-10		
Ruth 1:1-8		
Esther 4:10-17		
Daniel 3:1-18		
Daniel 6:4-22		
Acts 4:13-20		

Memorize: Philippians 3:10: "That I may know him, and the power of his resurrection, and the fellowship of his sufferings, being made conformable unto his death."

Prayer Time: Ask the Lord to help you trust Him for the unknown in your circumstances and decisions. Praise Him for revealing Himself to us through His Word that we may know Him!

CHAPTER 11—MORE THAN MY PAST AND PRESENT

The events of yesterday often shape our current life and ministries. Parts of our past we probably would rather forget. Maybe past decisions look foolish from today's perspective. We also have highlights in our life that are still a source of encouragement and accomplishment. God doesn't want us living in the past nor focusing on it more than we do on Him. The days at hand must also be kept in perspective. Are we living for the moment or for eternity?

How is the passing of time described in these verses?

Psalm 78:39

Psalm 90:9

What are we to realize about time?

>Psalm 39:4

>Psalm 90:12

>Proverbs 27:1

>2 Corinthians 6:2

>Ephesians 5:16

>Philippians 3:13-14

Memorize: Psalm 90:12: "So teach us to number our days that we may apply our hearts unto wisdom."

Prayer Time: Ask the Lord to help you trust Him for the unknown in your circumstances and decisions. Praise Him for revealing Himself to us through His Word that we may know Him!

CHAPTER 12—MORE THAN MY FUTURE

Tomorrow. What an impact it can have on today. It can steal our thoughts and energy and return us to reality feeling empty and hopeless. We miss today's opportunity to love and serve the Master.

Worry often is directly related to thoughts of the future. The unknown of tomorrow makes us doubt. How can we know what we will need tomorrow? It is unknown in spite of our efforts to plan ahead. Until it comes it's all unknown. Matthew chapter 6 gives us good instructions. Please read Matthew 6:19-34.

What are we not to worry about? (Matthew 6:25, 27)

What things from God's creation does Jesus use to help prove His care?

What words of comfort did Jesus give to those who could have worried? (v. 32)

What are we supposed to seek above all the necessary things of this world?

Where will our heart be? (Matthew 6:21)

Memorize: Matthew 6:33: "But seek ye first the kingdom of God, and his righteousness; and all these things shall be added unto you."

Prayer Time: Ask the Lord to help you trust Him for your daily needs. Praise Him for the excellent care He gives us.

CHAPTER 13—WHAT NOW?

Jesus commanded Peter to keep his focus on the service that God had called him to. Peter's focus was to be the nurturing of the lambs and sheep—both new and mature believers. Through the chapters of First and Second Peter, Peter challenges us to be ready for the suffering and trials that this life brings. Our salvation is firmly resting in the finished work of Jesus on the cross and His resurrection from the dead. We have a great hope to give to others! May we challenge those around us to "grow in grace, and in the knowledge of our Lord and Saviour Jesus Christ" (2 Peter 3:18).

How can you encourage those around you to "grow in grace and in the knowledge of our Lord and Savior Jesus Christ?"

How can you continue to grow as you should?

Who should you be praying for that fall into the category of the "lost," the "lambs," and the "loved?"

Read Titus 2:3-5. If you love God above all else, that love will spill over into the lives of people around you. Are you ready and willing to share that love? Who do you need to be a Titus 2:3-5 older woman for?

Memorize: 2 Timothy 3:14: "But continue thou in the things which thou hast learned and hast been assured of, knowing of whom thou hast learned them."

Prayer Time: Ask the Lord to show you who He would have you minister to. Begin to pray for opportunities to show His love to that person.

CHAPTER 14—THOU KNOWEST THAT I LOVE THEE

I hope this study has given you a better understanding of your love for God and His love for you. There are so many things that demand our affections. We can feel stretched beyond what we are capable of doing. My prayer is that these heartfelt thoughts that I have shared will challenge you to search your heart to honestly see the priority of your love and then make whatever adjustments are needed to love Him above all.

Read John 21 again and note the things you have learned from this account.

What did you realize to be the area that is easiest for you to put before your love for God?

What changes should you make in your life to keep your love for God in its proper place?

Memorize: Mark 12:30: "And thou shalt love the Lord thy God with all thy heart, and with all thy soul, and with all thy mind, and with all thy strength: this is the first commandment."

Prayer Time: Take a few minutes to pray asking the Lord to help you honestly evaluate the needs of your heart and your walk with Him. Praise Him for His great love for you!

Notes

CHAPTER 2

1. *The Pulpit Commentary*, Published circa 1890. Edited by H.D.M. Spence, D.D., Joseph S. Exell, M.A.
2. C.I. Scofield, *The Scofield Study Bible* (New York: Oxford University Press, 2003), 1424.
3. Charles H. Spurgeon, "Lovest Thou Me?" from *Sword Searcher.*

CHAPTER 5

1. Albert Barnes, *Notes on the New Testament,* Explanatory and Practical from *Sword Searcher.* Originally published 1832-1872.
2. D.L. Moody, Great Preaching of the Faith. "The Seven 'I Will's' of Christ." From *Sword Searcher.*

CHAPTER 7

1. John MacArthur, Jr., The MacArthur New Testament Commentary Matthew 16-23 (Chicago: Moody Press, 1988), p. 49.
2. Thomas Shepherd, "Must Jesus Bear the Cross Alone." *Rejoice Hymns* (Greenville, SC: Majesty Music, 2011), p. 287.
3. Isaac Watts, "When I Survey the Wondrous Cross." *Rejoice Hymns* (Greenville, SC: Majesty Music, 2011), p. 293.

CHAPTER 10

1. Thomas E. Ward, Sr., *Learning to Worship His Name* (Newark, DE: Partners in Ministry, 2012), i-ii.

For more information about
June Kimmel
&
More Than These

please visit:

junekimmel.wordpress.com
www.facebook.com/MoreThanThese
@JuneKimmel

For more information about
AMBASSADOR INTERNATIONAL
please visit:

www.ambassador-international.com
@AmbassadorIntl
www.facebook.com/AmbassadorIntl

*If you enjoyed this book, please consider leaving us a review on
Amazon, Goodreads, or our website.*

Made in the USA
Coppell, TX
25 April 2022